THE
WHISPERING
SOUL

Published in Ireland in 2009 by IPPS Ltd

Copyright © Betty Cosgrave, 2009

This Edition is Copyright © IPPS Ltd 2009

The Whispering Soul by Betty Cosgrave

The right of Betty Cosgrave to be identified
as the Author of the Work has been attested
by her in accordance with the Copyright,
Designs and Patents Act 1988.

A CIP catalogue record for this title is
available from the British Library.

ISBN 978-0-9562461-0-3

Cover and Book Design
by Philip Gambrill at Fresh Lemon.
Edited by Martin Roach
Printed in the Republic of Ireland by
Colourbooks Ltd

IPPS Ltd
Simmonscourt House
Simmonscourt Road
Ballsbridge
Dublin 4
Ireland

Tel: +353 1 2189201
Web: www.bettycosgrave.com
E-mail: info@bettycosgrave.com

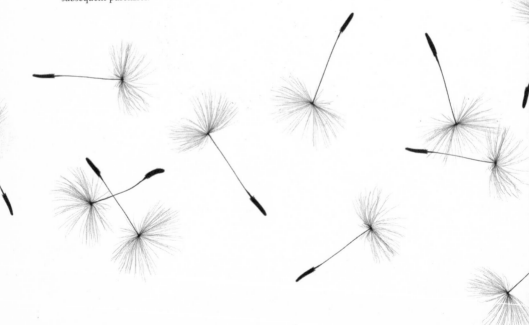

THE WHISPERING SOUL

BETTY COSGRAVE

IPPS LTD

ACKNOWLEDGEMENTS

There are a few people who I would like to thank for supporting me in the writing of *The Whispering Soul*. Dermot, my husband and best friend, my sons Fran, Gerry and Adam – thank you for all of your support and encouragement, I love you all so much. Josh, my little ray of sunshine from Liverpool – best grandson in the world. Martin Roach, an amazing editor, whose professional and personal advice was invaluable. Thank you for walking alongside me. My family; in particular my sister Eileen, for her feedback during the writing of this book. Phil Gambrill, for the wonderful artwork and design. Stephanie Parisot, whose amazing photographic skills produced the first photo of me that I have ever liked. David O'Neill for his great efforts in helping me get the book out there. Dave Henshaw for his sterling work on my website. Shelley Horan BCL for her legal guidance. My bank manager, Adele Delaney, for her unwavering support. Aine Carmody Smith, a very special friend, who not only gave me the benefit of her peerless P.R. skills but so much more besides. Linda Nicholson; thank you for your belief in me – it means a lot. All of the clients who allowed their case histories to be used, in the hope that others may be helped; in particular, my son Gerry who allowed me to share his challenge. And finally, a very special thank you to Kaye Roach, for the technical input and warm hospitality. Not forgetting Alfie Blue and Korda Ace who supplied the artwork for my kitchen.

Betty, September 2009.

CONTENTS

FOREWORD

I used to sit by myself on the little railing outside our house, watching the lane ... thinking. One day when I was only five, I saw a beautiful lady coming down the hill. I wasn't really aware of her actual age because I was a child, but I'd say she was probably in her late sixties. Her name was Kate and she was gorgeous but she was crippled with arthritis in her feet and hands. At first I just said 'Hello' but I saw her the next day as well and she stopped and we spoke some more. Over the next few days we started to look out for each other. She often came that way and I used to love seeing her, she was so kind and gentle to me. I used to wait excitedly at the top of the hill to see her and hold her hand.

The first time I actually helped her down the lane, I took her withered hand with my little fingers and she instantly spoke to me.

'Can you feel that, Betty? Can you feel that heat, that tingling? You're healing me.'

I wasn't really sure what she meant but I could feel the heat.

It came each time I held her hand or touched her twisted feet.

Each time I helped her down the lane.

I used to sit at the end of the lane and wait for her. My heart leapt when I saw her.

This went on for a few months and she used to say the most beautiful things to me.

'You are my little angel, Betty. That tingling is when we are exchanging energy, yours and mine. Look at my feet, they feel so much better. I love you, you are my little angel, you are a little goddess.'

'Is that what you see on a Christmas tree?' I asked.

'No, Betty,' Kate said with her kind and loving smile beaming down at me, 'a goddess is the most beautiful little spirit.'

That was the first time I became aware that I could do healing.

After about a year, I waited for Kate one day but she didn't come down the lane. I waited the next day too, but again she didn't come. Nor the day after or the one after that. She didn't come down the hill anymore.

I was on my own again.

As an adult, I now know that Kate's soul had passed through, because her journey in this life had come to an end.

But my healing – and my own journey – had only just started.

I find it strange that I sit here writing the Foreword to my own book. This is partly because until the age of 35, I could barely read or write. But it's also because at times I felt like I had nothing worth saying – or at least, that no one would listen if I did. However, despite my less than perfect circumstances growing up, I have been blessed with the opportunity to learn so many wonderful ways of looking at this beautiful journey we call life.

You are obviously interested in hearing some ideas too, because you hold this book in your hands. Well, you have already started work on one of the single most important points in here – taking responsibility yourself. So, well done, but there's plenty more to do!

I've split this book into four sections. Firstly, I'm going to tell you a little bit about myself, so that hopefully the tale of my life will show you why I needed to make changes and how I did that – with any luck, you'll pick up a few ideas for yourself along the way.

Secondly, I will explain my view of The Whispering Soul, why that is so important to your well-being and what that concept actually means; then I will take you through some simple but very powerful tips and techniques that you can try in order to make your life much more enjoyable. Finally, I shall share with you a few case histories of people that have worked with me. They had to discover how to manage their thoughts. I was able to help them do that because I had to learn to manage my own thoughts – I had no choice, I *had* to take charge.

If you can manage your thoughts too, then you have nothing to fear.

So go on, take a look.

What have you got to lose?

PART I

A MOST
BEAUTIFUL
LITTLE SPIRIT

CHAPTER I

LEDWIDGE CRESCENT

Our house was always dirty. Even as a young child, I wanted to clean it all the time. The house – in Ledwidge Crescent in the seaside town of Bray, County Wicklow – was infested with mice and the kitchen was their favourite place. They didn't even scurry away when you walked in, they were so used to wandering about. It was a typical house from an Irish council estate in the 1950s. When you came through the door, the stairs were to the left-hand side and opposite was the sitting room. At the back was the kitchen where we sat to eat. In there was also a little cupboard where we'd collect the coal – if we had any.

There was no central heating and no hot water. If you wanted a wash with hot water, it was a matter of lighting the fire. No fire? ... no hot water. Upstairs there was a bathroom and three small bedrooms. Most of the floors in the house had linoleum which was usually dirty. The garden was overgrown and overrun by vermin.

My mother was gone from early morning and wouldn't come home 'til late at night (my father was not around, but I'll come to him in a moment). So we took care of ourselves – in fact, my eldest sister took care of me a lot up until the age of probably five or six … I was dumped on her really. We didn't really sit down for meals together. We did very little talking, except for when there was arguments.

Even before we arrived at Ledwidge Crecent, my childhood had been less than straightforward. One of my earliest recollections is from our previous house in Wolfe Tone Square. I recall standing alone in the square in the middle of the night, wearing only a little vest. I was three years old. I'd gone to bed but woken up and gone downstairs looking to see if anyone was still awake. To me the house seemed empty. Being only three, I thought my sisters must be outside playing, so I opened the front door, walked down the path and through the gate into the street. Despite the poverty, in Wolfe Tone Square people didn't really close their doors and we didn't lock up at night. I went searching for my sisters. I vividly remember noticing how dark it was, pitch black, I couldn't tell the time obviously but it must have been very late at night. Eventually someone spotted me and knocked on a neighbour's door to tell my sister I was out in the street. As far as my sister was concerned, I was in bed and she had called in to visit her friend. She was still only a child herself, as I have said (as an adult I'd regularly dream about this incident, and in the dream I'd have blood all over my little vest, so it is obviously a distressing memory).

Why was I wandering the streets at night as a three-year-old, you might ask? Well, my mother was simply not always around. She was a gambler. However you look at it, in many ways it was abandonment but I know she often went away to get us food if she could. She worked several jobs: as a cleaner and at the railway station in the ladies toilets. That was all very hard work and she used to mind other people's children also. Then after work she'd usually go to the bingo or sit down at the slot machines. But she was a very hard worker.

When my mother had something, she'd give it away. She used to bring me down to the seafront with her and when she'd been working the slots for hours, she'd make me stand by a machine when she went for change and not let anyone else on. I was protecting the machine, 'Now, I'm here two hours, it's bound to come up with a win soon.' If that machine did come up with a win, there'd be a lot of goodies bought. A lot of goodies, nice stuff.

Yet my mother was not the sort of woman to show any affection, and I mean *any*. At least, not to us. As I sit and write this book, memories are waking up in me about experiences with my mother. I've just literally now remembered something that happened one day that I can see as clearly as if it was yesterday. It was early evening and I watched my mother come up the lane back from work. She must have won on the slots because she looked very happy. There were loads of kids in the street calling her 'Nanny Davis' and chatting to her and shouting and playing around her. And she was showing them a softness and affection that we rarely saw. I don't know why she couldn't show us that side of her, but the way she was with these other kids, it was lovely. I remember these kids running up and she was giving them sweets and they were saying 'Nanny Davis! We love you!' I watched this from my window and thought there must be something really wrong with me that she wasn't able to love me that way.

Her mother – my grandmother – was the same, she did not show us that kindness but I knew that other kids on the estate were spoken to in that gentle way. My grandmother used to take in children. Back then when children were born out of wedlock, the mother might have them taken away and given to someone else and that person was paid to mind them, often with no birth certificate. My grandmother had eleven of those children and four of her own. This was not that uncommon back then – several generations of Irish women had men in their lives that never stayed around. As the years went on, I realised that people loved my grandmother, but when it came to her own, she couldn't show any love or affection.

As I grew older, I began to see a different side to my mother too, she was a good woman, a strong woman, her circumstances were just very, very hard. They were both strong women with good hearts, they were just not able to make that connection with their own. My mother worked very hard and there is no doubt that she had a really kind heart, even though it was misplaced where I was concerned.

We'd moved to the house in Ledwidge Crescent when I was only four. Wolfe Tone Square was a poorer estate so when we got to Ledwidge Crescent, there were different types of family than what I was used to, those who would never have been on a housing estate before but maybe now couldn't afford their own houses because times were very hard. There were only a handful of families of what I would call 'my background' – by that I mean uneducated. Properly uneducated. Unable to read and write. My sisters were able to continue their friendships when we moved to the new estate but I hadn't really started any relationships like that because I was too young.

When we moved down from Wolfe Tone Square, we were followed a couple of months later by a family who moved in close to us. My mother was livid because she hated this woman and the arguments began almost immediately. For months my mother was saying, 'Oh, my God. We moved here to get away from her and now here she is, right on top of us.'

This lady would be saying things to upset my mother, such as 'You couldn't even hold on to your husband,' and 'You should stay at home and try looking after and feeding your children'. She would complain continuously about the dirt of our house and each morning when my mother would be going to work, she would be shouting things like, 'Where were you last night, Nan? Were you out ramblin' with the men again?' This ongoing row continued for at least fifteen years.

The mother of another neighbouring family, who would have been considered well off, especially compared to us, made it very clear that she didn't want her children associating with us, in any way, shape or form. Her husband was a seaman and would be away for months at a time. I can remember when he would be home, his wife would send him in to our door to complain about the dirt in our garden and how it was bringing rats and mice to the area. She was always complaining to the other neighbours about us too but it didn't make any difference and our house stayed the same. Welcome to Ledwidge Crescent.

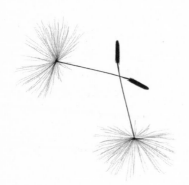

CHAPTER 2

MY LITTLE PIECE
OF SANCTUARY

I vividly remember my father repeatedly pinching me sharply and slapping me when I was only about three years old. It was in our very first house. I can see the room. It was quite dark and there were two chairs in it, this square, dingy room off a long hallway. My father wasn't around very much. Legally back then they didn't call it separated, but he lived in England and only came back probably once a year. To me that's separated. He worked in England, for the postal service I think. We had very little contact with him except maybe for two weeks a year, which was always horrible. He was really not a nice man.

Each time he came back, he was very cruel and everybody scattered. We were all in our own little units, protecting ourselves, you see. When I was very young I would be thrilled that he was coming home. I can remember telling the kids round by our house that he was coming and was going to bring me a doll, or something else nice. I told them that he was going to take me to the zoo, or other nice places. It was all a lie though, because he never brought me anywhere. Other kids had daddies and they came home from working away and played with them and everyone was happy. That's what I wanted. But that's not what I got. His behaviour was cruel and totally inappropriate.

My father was a very tall, skinny, red-haired man, with a very hard-face. He had glasses and always wore a suit. One of his legs would drag, but I never knew what was wrong. When he came back, he would maybe have a day and a half when he had money so he would go to the pub, then he would go home and sleep. He would smoke and the smell of his tobacco was horrendous to me. When he drank he would be a bit softer but when the drink wore off he'd be harder again and after that for the rest of the week I was in trouble, I was trapped.

He was a cruel and unkind man. He would beat me and say nasty things like I was the cause of all his problems. On several occasions he took me to Mass and stood me in church and said, 'There's God, there he is, and he knows that you are the cause of every problem we have.'

Then my dad would punish me when we got home.

I was left with him, I had no way out.

This is why I first started leaving my body.

The first time I remember was when he was home and was pinching me and slapping me and saying very cruel things to me. I had this terrible feeling of being trapped and I knew there was no one to rescue me, because my mother was at work and the others were all out. I can still recall the pain, even after all these years. I had no way out and then suddenly, there I was, 'up there' watching it all, floating … and I was laughing at him. The experience is exactly like watching something through a video camera. I was just an observer, floating up there. When I looked down I could physically see the back of his head over my body.

My soul had disconnected from my body.

I felt free.

As my disconnected soul watched my father beating me, I remember clearly thinking, *You can go back when he is gone. You are going to have to go back at some time.* I also remember reassuring myself, saying, *The person down there, it's okay, I'm minding us up here, so when I get back we'll make it okay.* It was like I became my own parent. That's exactly what it felt like.

Up there when I was observing what was going on, there was no pain … when the soul disconnects at that level, there is no mind, the physical, mental and emotional, no feelings of fear or sadness, it has all disconnected and it's just pure soul. I wasn't feeling anything.

When I disconnected from my body, it had a feeling of lightness. The best way I can describe it now is just feeling no connection to this earth, being just a floating, free spirit, feeling the freedom to watch the events unfolding in that room but not having to connect with them.

And above all, I felt absolutely *safe*.

Why was this happening?

I would never let them touch my soul.

At an early age I was very aware of my soul and very conscious of the need to protect my soul, even before I went to school. This sense became more and more acute as I got older. My soul was too precious to me, so what I would do is I would leave my body and watch it happening from a safe distance.

My father wasn't hurting my soul. He couldn't touch it. My soul was safe.

At the same time, I also knew that at some point I would have to go back into myself. When he left the room, I just floated down and engaged back in the body. People often ask me what it feels like to literally re-engage back into your own body – well, the best way I can describe it is there's a gentleness and a softness and then suddenly I'm back in.

What is easy to describe, however, is the feeling of sadness that would then envelop me very quickly afterwards. I felt very sad and frightened and I felt this stranger – I called him my daddy but I hadn't seen him for a year – was here, hurting me and there was nobody to mind me. This stranger who was given the name Daddy was a very angry man. This all made me very sad.

After he had stopped hurting me, I'd just curl up on the seat with my knees pulled to my chest and just rock back and forth.

Back and forth.

Back and forth.

Over and over.

I'd go into this place where I would just 'be' again. Some people call that meditation – I wouldn't have known that term then, but that's what people might call it. I would switch off again but this time I'd stay in my body.

Having spoken to members of my family since, I now know that people saw me doing this and were – understandably perhaps – concerned, that they felt there was clearly something wrong with me. Had a doctor seen me doing that rocking back and forth at that time, they would have thought there was something very wrong indeed.

Once I switched back out of that meditative state and the entire episode had passed, I'd come back very loud. There was such a feeling of being alone in my childhood that when I came out of that state – and I know this might sound strange – that I literally didn't know if people could physically *see* me or not. To me it was perfectly natural to separate my soul from my body so it seemed reasonable to wonder if people couldn't actually see me. I compensated by being super loud and super attention-seeking. Of course they could see me, but that seed of doubt in my mind meant I made sure I was visible by being noisy. My sister often said I would drive them mad at these times. I was an horrendous attention seeker and would sometimes hurt myself on purpose – not to self-harm, just to get attention.

One particular incident shows you how much I would crave attention at these times. I think I was about six.

I put a ruler in my mouth and ran down the stairs and into the wall.

I remember screaming with the pain. My sister took the ruler out of my throat and said, 'Oh, you'll be grand.' I was bleeding but it was always 'Oh, you'll be grand.' That's what we did in my family, we didn't do pain, it was always 'Oh, you'll be grand.' Everything is grand. If you had a pain in your ear from an ear infection … 'You'll be grand.' So that day my sister just smoothed over the mark and said, 'Yes, it's bleeding a bit but it'll clear, you'll be grand.'

But I wasn't grand.

At a very young age, I was used to being on my own. One day I heard about somebody who had died, an older gentleman from around the corner. I also heard everybody would be going to the church and I realised that there'd be lots of people there so I thought I'd go and have a look. There was a little hole in the graveyard wall so I ducked through that and immediately saw a group of people dressed in black, many of whom were crying. I watched what was going on from a short distance.

My first thought was that this emotion they were showing, feeling – I didn't know at this point it was called grief – was something that I was familiar with. Although at this young age I hadn't actually been bereaved yet, I did carry a sense of grief inside me. I could identify with their grief. The people grieving made me feel a little bit more secure somehow with what I had been feeling. Whatever it was, these people were feeling it too.

There was a grief hiding inside of me.

Then I noticed one particular lady standing with a small group of people and she was crying. There was a man standing next to her who seemed to know her and he was talking to her, but she wasn't listening, or at least wasn't answering.

After a while, he turned towards me and said, 'Can she hear me?'

That's when I realised it was his funeral.

It felt *completely* normal for him to speak with me, so I answered him.

'She doesn't seem to hear you.'

'But I want to tell her something …'

'What do you want to tell her?' I asked.

'That I've left too soon and that I am sorry, I wasn't supposed to go yet.'

I could hear him and see him as clearly and as definitely as the people who were at the funeral grieving for him. Talking to him was the same as talking to anybody else.

It just didn't seem strange to me.

'Touch her on the shoulder …' I suggested, out loud.

He did but his wife didn't notice. We chatted some more and then he walked away, following the crowd of mourners.

When I went home that evening, I felt completely normal. I was consciously aware that he wasn't alive, that he was a spirit but other than that it was a totally normal and understandable conversation for me to have had.

The next day I went back to the graveyard to see if he was still there. He was and we chatted some more. He told me that he'd followed his wife all the way home. On the fourth day, we were chatting when a big, bright light appeared. It looked so inviting and warm and I said, 'I think I know that light, what is it? Can I go through there?'

'No, you can't I'm afraid, it isn't your time,' he answered.

'But what is it?'

'Sometimes we go through the light straight away and sometimes it takes us a little while.'

Then he just went into a shadow in front of me and was gone.

I started seeing spirits pretty frequently from around the age of five. It didn't seem strange to me. It never occurred to me that this wasn't ordinary. I hadn't made any connections with kids on the new estate, I was too cut off from reality to make friendships. At home and on the estate I felt I was on the wrong planet. I'd felt so different from the age of about four. I couldn't make connections anywhere with anything or anyone. My family being so disjointed made it worse, of course. Even seeing souls, I didn't tell anyone because we didn't talk anyway. I didn't feel the need to tell anyone because I was experiencing so many things that I wasn't telling anybody about anyway.

I'd rather make friendships with what I perceived to be the ghosts that were around me and the spirit world. I was much happier there, there was more kindness and security. Very quickly I found myself drawn to the graveyard in the hope that one of the spirits I saw there would take me with them.

I used to think, *One of them will bring me back with them, I'll be able to go home with them … wherever they are going.* I felt such *warmth* towards the souls. I felt drawn to going with them.

I wasn't asking to die. I didn't think about that. I wasn't consciously aware of death in that way. Even though I was in the graveyard, the concept of dying or not dying didn't register. The concept for me was to be in a place where I was comfortable. Where there didn't appear to be any pain, where there seemed to be great release, where there was some sort of safety … yes, that's the word … safety.

It's hard to recall exactly how often I would see souls. My time-frame as a child wasn't very clear, but it could have been days or maybe weeks before I saw souls at the graveyard again. Most times I would hear of someone dying in the estate and I'd go to the funeral. Sometimes I'd just go there because I had so much spare time alone. Unlike most five-year-olds, nobody would come looking for me no matter how long I was out of the house, so I'd just go there and see who I could meet. I got in a habit.

There was always talk about deaths on the estate, about people dying and I would hear this and be so excited about going to the graveyard when there was the funeral. I knew that I would see the spirit of the person that had died and I knew that I would get to talk to them. There was a *connection* and that was something that was badly lacking in my 'relationships' with the people in my life. So I was totally drawn to those circumstances because I felt comfortable.

By startling contrast, my dad would still take me to Mass when he was back and the same cruelty would return. He would stand me in church and say, 'You see the man on the cross, he knows you make me do bad things, he knows how evil you are.'

I was five years old.

I know I was very young but I remember thinking to myself, as I stood there in my little coat, *He's not my God, he's your God. My God's lovely and he says I'm lovely. I know a beautiful God that loves me and I'm a lovely little girl and I am not bad. And I've already been in touch with souls and spirits and angels and I know that I am not bad.*

The souls became my little piece of sanctuary.

As I spoke with these souls more and more, I learned that what the first soul had referred to as 'a little while' before spirits go through the light, was in fact three days. During this three-day period, certain souls cannot move across; on the fourth day they will go through the light if they have been able to resolve any problems or unfinished business. Other souls would just be gone over within those three days.

However, some wouldn't go over after the three days was up, they would stay and I would chat with them for long periods of time. They may be souls who had unfinished business. A lot of people ask me what a soul 'looks like'. If they have no unfinished business, for the actual three days they look exactly the same as a living person to me, except with no shadow. After that period, if they haven't passed through, it would be like a silhouette of themselves. There was one particular soul who I would just find in the churchyard walking up and down, up and down, constantly walking, he didn't talk to me but he was there all the time. I didn't get any communication, he was stuck for whatever reason. However, most would eventually vanish only to be replaced by new souls.

I started getting more familiar and started asking more questions of them. I also asked them on many occasions to go through the light with them but they always said no. Gradually I realised that I was going to be left here. Although this wasn't what felt safe and natural to me, I gradually accepted being here.

But the visits to the graveyard did not stop.

CHAPTER 3

SWITCHING OFF

I had glimpses of kindness as a child. Kate – the arthritic old lady who'd called me a goddess – was one wonderful little episode for me. Then, around the age of seven, a neighbour across the road had a visit from the family of one of their brothers. He'd gone to England and married a lovely lady called Patricia and they had two young children. I will never forget her, she was like an angel; there was a bright light around her. She was the most beautiful individual and thankfully for a short while she took me under her wing.

I was pushy in the beginning. She was right across the road and I was so curious to meet her. The first day she arrived, the kids were out playing in the street so I went over to her and she said, 'Who's in there with you?' and I said, 'Nobody' and without a moment's pause she said, 'Well, come on over and play with us then.' And from that day onwards, she was like an angel to me.

She was amazing, very soft. I would go for walks with her, she cooked lovely meals and I ate with her every day and played with the children as much as I could. She was light, she would sing, she would dance, she would talk. She would teach me about girls' clothes and even buy me little shoes. She stayed for about a year and a half and that was probably the best 18 months of my young life. Oh God, she was so beautiful.

In the meantime, while she was living over the road, there were times when our electricity was cut off. As if that wasn't bad enough, periodically the rent man would come and shout through the letterbox 'If your mother doesn't pay next week tell her she will be evicted!' I didn't even know what the word 'evicted' meant but the shouting frightened me.

Yet while Patricia was there, none of that mattered. Sometimes I would stay with her at night, if my sisters were with friends and my mother was out (which was a lot). All of a sudden there was a safety net that hadn't been there before.

I remember thinking to myself, *Wow, this is the way I want to live when I grow up, not the other way. I will never live the other way.*

Then Patricia went back to England and it all stopped overnight.

Despite, or perhaps because of the lack of kindness, I was always looking to make a connection with people around me. I had that very deep connection with the souls I saw at the graveyard, but I still struggled to make a connection elsewhere. By the time I was eight, I was consciously aware that I needed to make some personal connections, that it wasn't great to grow up without any. So I started putting on little plays for the kids on the estate. We had a big table in the sitting room and there was a window next to it. I used to get some material and tie the curtains from the window to the door to make a little seating area and then charge children a farthing or whatever to come and see my little productions. They used to queue out the door!

Despite my circumstances, I believe I was a lovely kid at this age. I was kind and caring and very gentle. I enjoyed bringing all the local kids into the play and putting on a little show. Sometimes I used to wrap a piece of blue material around me and pretend I was Our Lady and if I was feeling mischievous I'd get them to say prayers and then jump out the window, which they couldn't see because the curtain covered it, then jump back in through the door and surprise them all! It was all lovely, innocent fun and looking back I was the proper little businesswoman, making a few coins here and there. I had a much older mind in my head. But even from a child's perspective, I came *alive* when I did those plays. I was being accepted, there were all these people around and it was fun. It was actual *fun*.

From as young as five, I'd get myself ready for school along with my sisters. If there was anything around for lunch, we'd make a sandwich; if there wasn't anything, we'd eat nothing. They might give us a bun and some milk at school. There was a uniform and we had that, but it was not very clean most of the time, it wasn't washed that much and it often went on wet.

School was the other side of Bray, so it was probably about two miles through the town. We got there by ourselves which might sound bad but to be fair a lot of kids from our background would have gone to school and come home themselves. All of the other kids on the estate went to a local school which was only five minutes away, and so were all very friendly with each other but because I went to school so far away, it just helped add to my feeling of isolation. When I was very young, someone used to bring my sisters to school – I can't remember who exactly – but she'd stick me in a pram as well and wheel me along with them.

School did not make my circumstances better, it was no haven for me or my sisters. From a very young age, I would come home from school with my hands bleeding where the teacher had smacked me with the side of a ruler to 'bring me back'. She had a cane too. The problem was I used to 'switch off' too many times. The teachers called me a day-dreamer but that's not what I would call it. I would just not be present, not present at all, my body was in class but I was floating off around school, watching some kids doing PE or whatever, then I would come back into my body later.

Fortunately, sometimes in my unconscious I would be able to pick up things the teacher was saying, so if I was singled out for a question I might just be able to answer it. I couldn't write but if it was a verbal answer I might be okay. The reading and writing I just couldn't grasp, because that takes focus and I couldn't focus, I kept leaving myself. Sometimes I got away with it and they thought I was paying attention after all and on those occasions they'd leave me alone. Other times, they'd see I wasn't 'there' and out would come the ruler.

I would get punished for 'switching off', but my sisters didn't have it easy either. I remember one day the teacher made fun of my sister and I. Well, 'making fun' doesn't really cover it. She banged my sister's head off the wall and took her around the class saying, 'Look, these are the stupid children.' Her ear was bleeding. That's the way they looked at us. But the problem was there was nobody to take up for us, there was no one going to correct the teachers or stand up for us. We had no parents to intervene when things like this happened.

Periodically when I was fully present, I would be very boisterous and would go all out to become friends with somebody at school, ideally to go home with them. I would crave going home with someone where there was a parent who made dinner and there was electricity on, maybe the dad was lighting a fire, where everything appeared to be normal. So I would go all out to try to get in with little groups of children and I'd be very clever and pick someone who was maybe not completely in with the rest of the group. Then once I'd befriended them, I would go to their house to play and maybe eat some food. Unfortunately, although I would make friends with them, the parents would very quickly stop my visits because I was unkempt and because of where I was coming from. I would usually get one visit then the parents would realise.

'Oh, is somebody not coming for you?'

'No, I'll go by myself.'

'But you live way back there? How will you get back home?'

'Oh, I go back home by myself all the time.'

And that would be the end of that.

There were also long periods of time when I didn't go to school at all and I would get away with it. I might go into school but then I'd sneak off. A lot of the time they'd be glad that I was gone, because I was very unkempt and I was trouble. Or if I wasn't trouble I was out of my body and not even present and I would cause a disturbance. Schools were so very, very different back then. I'd got very clever and capable so on many occasions I would sneak out, go home and close the curtains and stay inside … and just go into myself. I remember one period when I didn't go to school for quite a while – in my perception it seemed like months but it might have been just weeks. Eventually the police came for me.

I remember this face looking through the letterbox. He called out to me for a while and eventually I replied.

'I can't let you in.'

'But you have to let me in, who is there with you?'

'I'm here myself.'

'Why did you not go to school today?'

'I'm sick.'

'If you're sick, who's there with you?'

'Oh, they're coming back in a few minutes.'

'Okay, I'll wait.'

He came back two hours later and there'd be nobody home yet so he said, 'I'm going to have to come in and get you if you don't open the door.'

I opened the door and he took me back to school.

Even then, they didn't take it any further. Back in those days, there were a lot of families like us and the regulations were virtually non-existent compared to the modern day. During my earlier years, the authorities were barely involved at all, it wasn't like it is today. The only real 'official' involvement we had came from something called The Humane Society. They would periodically send people into the house to clean it up. The place was very dirty, as I have said, mice and filth everywhere, so they'd come in every so often and clean us out. There were no questions asked and no intervention of any kind.

Then they'd just go away again.

CHAPTER 4

THE END OF A FANTASY

My father used to send home a telegram each week with some money for my mother. It was only something small, but by the time I was about six, he'd stopped sending anything at all.

I wanted a daddy so much. A daddy who would love me and treat me like a princess. All I had was a fantasy and that caused me even more pain. His annual visits continued and so did the beatings and extreme cruelty. Each visit I still wondered if he would take me to the zoo this time, maybe buy me a doll this time and I'd get excited, but then when he sometimes never even showed up, the kids on the estate would tease me mercilessly, which meant that I ended up staying in the house and withdrawing into myself even more.

I remember one day when I was twelve, walking into my hall to answer a knock on the front door. I immediately got a smell that I hadn't sensed for a couple of years. It was my father's tobacco. I was thrown into a panic instantly. My heart was pounding. My whole body started shaking and I felt as if I had been punched in the head. I fell to the floor and started rocking involuntarily. This had started happening fairly regularly by this age. Sometimes it happened when I was out in the streets and people didn't know it was a panic attack at the time so they'd think I was having a heart attack. I literally couldn't breathe.

I don't know how long I was rocking on the floor, but by the time I was able to open the door, my father had become very aggressive because he'd been left standing so long on the step. I told him that my mother wouldn't be home until later and then I ran straight out of the house, to escape him.

I walked around for hours and eventually ended up in the graveyard. I hadn't really been there since I was about seven because I'd realised as I grew older that I didn't need to physically be there to speak with spirits. I went straight to my special spot in the oldest part of the graveyard. It was where I felt most comfortable and I sat there for hours until I thought that my mother would be home and it would be safe for me to go back.

Unfortunately though, when I got in she wasn't there and my father was still very angry and aggressive. He demanded that I make him a sandwich because he was hungry. While I was doing that, my mother arrived, went into the front room and closed the door. Shortly afterwards I heard her shouting, 'No! No! I will not do that!' Then she left the house and was gone for a long time but when she returned, the shouting began all over again. It turned out that he wanted to separate from her and she wasn't having it. She told him that it was hard enough already because he had left her and people were talking about how she couldn't hold a husband so she wasn't going to make it official by agreeing to a separation.

He stayed for two nights and was really cruel to me. He told me that I was ugly. He said I had always been ugly and he even said that I wasn't actually his daughter. In fact he said none of the kids were his. I had to listen to his ranting for two days before he left.

He didn't turn up again for about two years. It was a repeat performance of the last visit but the difference was that I was stronger and wasn't prepared to take any of his crap. I threw everything back at him. I gave him as good as I got and it infuriated him. This time he was mostly verbally and mentally cruel, he was saying really nasty things but I was older and I knew I didn't have to be bullied by him. I'd just say, 'I'm not listening. I am not what you say I am. I am not a bad person. I am a good person,' and then I'd leave. It made him so angry but I wasn't prepared to be bullied any more. His stay only lasted three days and still my mother wouldn't agree to his demand for a separation.

The next time I saw him was eleven years later, on his death-bed in England.

CHAPTER 5

A WORLD APART AND THE SUPERMARKET OWNER'S SON

When I'd started secondary school, questions were quickly asked about my health. The school was much better than my horrible primary. So, on the one hand, all of a sudden I had teachers paying attention to me and wanting to teach me. However, I couldn't actually hear what they were saying. I didn't know why but I just couldn't hear. Obviously I'd never had any tests or investigations regarding my health but one particular teacher took an interest in me and decided that something had to be done. He was called Mr McCoy and he was this big, beautiful man who took a shine to me.

I was lucky in a way because I was very aware I was a demon at times. I was very precocious and cheeky but yet I was very direct and he liked that and took it upon himself to help me. He said, 'I have to get you down to the clinic.' He knew something wasn't right so he got me seen by an expert. They ran some tests and the results showed that I had only 15% hearing in my left ear. They said that my ear-drum was severely perforated and had obviously suffered multiple untreated infections. Basically, over the years, these various infections had eaten away at my ear-drum to the point where I was effectively going deaf. Once that was diagnosed, I was given a prescription straight away and my hearing did start to improve.

Then aged just thirteen, my gums started bleeding profusely. It was terrible. Again Mr McCoy intervened and arranged for me to be seen by a local dentist but unfortunately that was where the caring stopped. Back then, dentists weren't so kind and this particular man was very rough. My teeth were rotten, you see, so he just ripped them all out. The bleeding became far worse, it was gushing for days after, so then he said that my blood wasn't clotting properly and there were signs of potential blood poisoning. So it was decided to plug the holes where he'd ripped my teeth out. He did this but the plugs only lasted three months and the bleeding continued anyway. After the three months, he pulled those plugs out and put some new ones in and so it went on for a year, put the plugs in, rip them out, I was more or less a year with no teeth.

During that year, Mr McCoy took me to one side one day and said, 'You're not going to make it here, Betty, are you? What is happening with your teeth?' I told him that they'd been plugging the gaps but other than that, nothing.

'Have they not come back to you with a date for your false teeth to be fitted, Betty?'

'No, Sir, they haven't.'

'Come into the office with me Betty,' he said. I followed him in where he phoned the dentist there and then. I had the false teeth within a month.

He was the first teacher who had ever taken care of me.

School was okay after that for a while. Then a few terms later, Mr McCoy took me into his office again and sat me down before turning to me and gently saying, 'Betty, I know you are doing very well and you are remembering things and coming forward, and I know that many of the teachers say you are doing really well and seem okay.'

'Yes, Sir.'

'But it's all false isn't it, Betty?'

He was right. I was putting on a brave face.

'Look, we will get you a job. My sister owns a newsagent in Shankill and there's a little job there helping out with the newspapers.'

This was very unusual because the common thing at the time for a girl of my background and age was to work in a factory. But the newsagents sounded great so I went along – now bear in mind that at this point in time I couldn't read or write. Mr McCoy said he would help me by colour coding the newspapers so I knew which ones to organise. I pretended I could read and he didn't tell his sister, plus I was good at faking it by now so even if there was a form I'd get someone else to fill it in and tell me what it said.

I hated the job.

The problem was his sister wasn't kind like Mr McCoy. Because I couldn't read or write, I kept making mistakes and she wasn't very kind when I did. Nevertheless, it was a job and I stayed there for almost a year.

I was becoming really unwell. Around this time I had a manic episode at my sister's house – she was married with children by this stage. She lived in Little Bray, I went down to her and I really wasn't well. I had a pain in my stomach and my head and I was screaming. I couldn't stop the pain and there were voices. She brought me to a doctor.

During his examination, the doctor said, 'Did somebody hurt you?'

I couldn't talk and I wouldn't say anyway, so I said, 'Nobody hurt me, but there's a voice in my head,' and I started screaming again. 'There's a pain in my head, Doctor, it's so bad, it's like someone sticking a knife in me.'

'Did somebody hurt you or do something to you, Betty?'

'No, no.'

After two days of seeing me, he diagnosed me with depression.

Something else happened around this time too, that was to be a turning point for me. One day, these two boys came in, they were two years older than me, maybe even seventeen and they were both working. One of them was really handsome, with long, blond hair and he was beautiful looking but it was the other guy who fancied me! I wasn't good-looking but I was aware I had something, I was bouncy and even obnoxious at times but I had *something*. His friend really fancied me and kept coming in but not buying anything so eventually I said, 'What do you want?' and he said, 'I want to ask you out!' and I said, 'But I fancy your mate!'

Even though his beautiful mate didn't fancy me, it was the beginning of a new chapter in my life. I had a small job, my teeth were fixed, my hearing was reasonable, and here I was enjoying chats with these lads coming into the shop flirting around me. That was a new cycle in my life starting.

A few hundred yards down the road from the newsagents was a handbag factory and after about a year I went to work there. This was a world apart from the newsagents, I loved it. I loved the smell of the leather and I loved making things. I didn't have to use my head – or at least my academic head –

I had to use my eyes and my creative energy. And I found that I was good at it. I sat there and made beautiful handbags and sometimes I'd be so proud of what I'd done that I'd just sit there and look at them. That was another corner turned, I had a job I enjoyed and work that I was proud of.

I was into my mid-teens by now and boys were obviously something that interested me! I'd asked my sister if I could go to the local dance but she'd said no, so I asked another girl who, like me, struggled to make friends. We both got all dressed up and sneaked off to our first dance. The two lads from the newsagents were there and your man who kept asking me out was chatting away to me but I wasn't having it. I wanted the beautiful one. What's more, he had a motorbike!

But he didn't even see me.

At least, I thought he didn't even see me.

I kept trying to chat to him and eventually we did get talking and had a nice time (much to the annoyance of his friend). He took me home at the end of the dance and we chatted some more and then he said goodnight and went away.

He came to me the next day and asked me out, I was so excited!

I ended up being in and out of a relationship with the beautiful boy with the motorbike – Steve – for years.

Away from Steve and the handbags and the local dance and my lively personality though, I was very sick. From a very young age, I would use food to deal with issues. At such a young age, you obviously aren't aware of why you are doing it but initially I used to steal food because there was frequently nothing in the house. If my mother hadn't paid her bills there'd be no food in the house so I'd go to the shop to get something. The shop was like a very early mini-supermarket, with shelves of old-fashioned sweets on the right-hand side and a sloping counter with more sweets and bread at the front. At the very front of the counter they had a stand with all these tins of broken biscuits. You'd ask for some and say how much money you had, then the shop-keeper would weigh out what he could give you.

Back then you'd have credit in shops. I'd ask for something and they'd go into the back to look up our account and I'd wait and wait and wait. I knew they'd say my mother hadn't paid up to date, so quite often I'd wait until the man went out the back and slip some broken biscuits into this little bag I used to carry around.

I would take the biscuits back to the house and hide them, then when I was upset or angry or couldn't cope, I'd eat. The biscuits were kept for when I was hurting. It helped my emotional pain.

I've since gone back to that shop and apologised for my behaviour.

In my early teens I used food but then when I hit fifteen I found alcohol. I would use alcohol to blank me out periodically. It suppressed me. Going back to my home … it was still not a nice place to live, it really wasn't.

I became friendly with the sister of Steve, the guy I was dating. I also made friends with his mother and spent a lot of time at their house. They lived out in Greystones and it was a lovely home. Oh God, to me it was amazing to see and be a part of that home. They cooked dinners and all sat down together to eat and talk. For a while there I had another home. I'd get the bus and then it was a 40-minute walk but I didn't mind at all; I'd be able to go out to his parents and I got on brilliant with his mother. The whole lot of them, in fact.

When I compare this to what my own home life was like, it was no wonder I was searching for something else. I remember one night, a friend from work stayed over with me. A relative was visiting and came home after we had gone to bed and he was drunk. Knowing that I had a friend staying over, this man came upstairs and started banging on my bedroom door, shouting that we were lesbians and then all sorts of twisted stuff. He was banging and kicking the door but luckily it was locked. My friend was so terrified and upset by it all that she tried to jump out of the window and run away. I calmed her down and apologised and she said, 'Betty, how do you live here?'

I would yo-yo between highs and lows regularly. The highs manifested themselves in many ways. For example, I might rush out and buy loads of clothes that wouldn't even fit me. I would compulsively shop and my older sister would find it odd because I'd often buy clothes that were too small for me, something I can now see was tied in to my issues with food. Other times I'd buy clothes that were too big for me. I might in my own head think I was bigger than I was and buy something too large (later, when I was pregnant with my first child Fran, I thought I was really fat; the scars from my teenage years mean I lost the concept of reality around size and weights. The strange thing was that I came across a photo of myself recently, which was taken while I was pregnant with Fran and I was shocked to see that I wasn't actually overweight at all). I never got things to fit me. That was just an escape, like any other form of escapism. It became a compulsion.

Then when a low came it would be a very deep low and I'd often just sit in my bedroom in the dark, not go to work and listen to Leonard Cohen, rocking back and forth, back and forth again.

By now my sisters had gone from the house. My oldest sister went to live in Scotland for a while and another one went to live in England. It was just myself and my brother and mother left in the house.

I was still seeing Steve and usually we had a lovely time. His family said we were meant to be together, they were great.

I had made a connection with his sisters and had glimpsed a way of living that was so completely different and better than what I was used to. They were a very close family.

Unfortunately, me and Steve were on and off a lot. We had a deep soul connection but I was still very sick, I was not a well person. I was very up and down and extremely insecure. I had dreadfully low self-esteem. On one particular occasion I decided I had to get away from it all and move to England. Eileen, one of my aunts, got in touch with another aunt who lived in London and arranged for me to go and stay with her. She even bought me a ticket for the boat. Even though I was nervous about the move, I knew in my heart that I had to break away, so off I went to see what England held in store for me.

My 'aunt' was called Edie and she was actually one of the children that my grandmother had taken in. Now I have to tell you that Edie was a stunningly beautiful woman. Her DNA had given her the most striking elegance and good looks. We didn't actually know where her DNA came from because she had no birth certificate. My grandmother had been very cruel to Edie and so she had got away at a very young age but because of a lack of education and opportunity, she couldn't get a job easily. Luckily she met a beautiful, older man who fell completely in love with her and looked after her.

I went to stay with Edie and a whole other new chapter in my life began. Edie had a gorgeous home, where she lived with her son. You walked in through a beautiful big door that was covered in this splash of lovely glass, through into a hallway full of antique furniture. The garden was fabulous, it was all kept immaculate, like a five-star hotel, it really was a totally different world to what I was used to.

When I arrived at Edie's home on the Edgware Road, I was struck by how different she was to what I was used to. She was so beautiful and seemed so confident. It was a revelation for me. She promised to teach me how to be in 'normal' society and took me to a wonderful restaurant. I had never seen a proper place-setting before and was shocked by the amount of cutlery on the table. She explained all about starting from the outside in and how to order from a menu. When she realised that I had difficulty with reading, she had a solution for that as well. She told me that I should look over the menu and then ask the waiter for his recommendation, so I wouldn't feel uncomfortable. She took me to many different restaurants and explained that I needed to be comfortable with all of this because I would be meeting lots of new people and it was best for me to be comfortable in these situations.

She was a fantastic lady and I loved my time with her so much. In fact she got me a job in a local supermarket. I started work there and within a couple of weeks I'd made a few friends. One of them, Joe, was about a year older than me. He came from a completely different background to mine, in as much as his father was a doctor, his mother was a lawyer and his sister was studying law at university. Joe had had a breakdown from being bullied in school, so his parents had got him this job to try and help him build up his confidence. They were amazing people. One night they invited myself and two others from the supermarket to join them for dinner at their home. I was so glad that Edie had shown me how to use cutlery because the dinner was a proper affair, with a full table setting. Their dining room was like a fine restaurant. The family spoke to me as though I was an equal and I was so struck by the way in which they supported Joe.

I made some amazing friends at the supermarket. I was on the Deli counter and although my very poor reading skills could have held me back, I made sure it didn't. I was bubbly with all the customers and I worked very hard. My employers were very good too – they could see I had problems with reading but they could also see I was good at my job and they supported and encouraged me. Every day I would arrive earlier than I had to and leave later than was expected.

At home, Edie really took me under her wing and helped me so much. She started to dress me and show me how I could wear clothes nicely. And she did all of this even though she was still getting herself well from her own difficult childhood. She was so kind to me.

Edie was – like Steve's family, like Mr McCoy, like Patricia and like Kate – a glimpse of another way of life. The way she spoke to me, helped me, advised me and looked after me was wonderful.

Unbeknown to me, two of my new friends from the supermarket, Anne and Sarah, would introduce me to a way of life that is still with me to this day in one form or another – meditation. I didn't know what that even was at this point, but I got chatting to them one day and they invited me along to a meditation group. I went along and they were really nice people, they made me feel very welcome.

I quickly realised this was in fact what I had been doing since I was very little.

That particular meeting was a spiritual group and in that very first chat, they actually talked about souls passing over to the other side and people who go before their time. They also talked about how we can help souls who are struggling to pass over. I was sitting there literally hearing people talk about things that had been happening in my life since I was very young.

I felt like I'd arrived home.

I started attending meditation classes with Joe and after a while, his parents began to invite me to come for lunch on Sundays. I became very friendly with them and my confidence started to grow. It was a very good period in my life and probably the first time I knew what it was like to be happy. While I still felt a bit insecure, I had stopped having panic attacks and didn't feel the need to escape from my life like I used to. I started getting to know what I would call the 'soul me'. I began to see a lovely future. The power of the past began to weaken. It didn't own me as much. I know now that I was listening to my soul whispering …

Steve was still in touch with me at this point – he'd been heartbroken when I left for England and kept getting in touch. After six months, Steve came over to England to visit me. I could see Edie was anxious about the visit and she took me to one side and said, 'Now, Betty, don't even think of going back over with him, will you? You must not go back. I see you really love him but I can't see it working out for you…'

Steve arrived in England on the Friday evening and first thing Saturday morning I handed in my notice at the supermarket and broke the news to Edie that I was going back to Ireland. The thing was, I loved Steve to bits and he loved me. And it wasn't like I was exactly an easy girlfriend for him, oh my God, far from easy now. I was quite a disturbed person, I am very aware of that, I had an awful lot of issues. I would be clingy and low, yet in other ways I'd be bouncy and great fun. Even with the progress I'd made in England, I was still not an easy option for him, but he loved me.

I went back home with Steve and within a week I realised I'd made a dreadful mistake.

Almost as soon as I'd arrived back, I started falling back into my old patterns. Then Eileen, the aunt who bought me the ticket over to London, died in a tragic accident. She had fallen asleep one night with the gas fire turned on but the meter had run out, however someone else coming in later that night had put money in the meter and Eileen died in her sleep as a result. Edie came over for her funeral and spoke to me afterwards, asking me to return with her. I was very tempted but I'd started a new job, so I promised to think about it.

I never saw Edie again after that day, but I will be forever grateful to her for the vision she gave me.

When I'd left London, the supermarket manager there had very kindly given me an amazing reference so I was able to get a job quite quickly in the Stillorgan branch of a supermarket chain called Quinnsworth. Despite my deteriorating state of mind, to some degree I could manage there okay. After all, I'd got so much experience hiding the fact I couldn't read or write very well, from employers and customers. I'd developed that into quite a skill. I'd made friends at the supermarket and we'd always go out at weekends to the pub and I'd sometimes drink a little more than I should have and then vow not to drink again for ages. Then I'd settle down a bit, see lots of Steve and go out for nice meals with his sisters, but I would always have an underlying discomfort; there was an unease about my life and I think this was what I was trying to blank out during the times when I drank. Matters were made worse at home because my mother was not well by this stage. She'd become addicted to valium and was very under-weight, and she was struggling in her own self. Much of her life she'd been very over-weight, maybe 15 or 16 stone. Then after she became addicted to valium, her weight dropped dramatically, to the point where it was so noticeable that a doctor actually rang the family and implied that she was malnourished and wasn't being looked after properly. She went from one extreme to the other.

It's easy to see now why moving back to Ireland was such a bad decision. Nothing had changed. My home was still very dysfunctional. The temptation to go out drinking was there. I was away from Edie and all the steadying influence and kindness that she provided. I tried to change things at home – I was earning good money so I used some of my wages to put in a new fireplace and a tank for hot water (not central heating, this just made hot water) and I was constantly cleaning. Having come from Edie's house, it was quite a shock to walk back through the door at home, so I tried to make it more like what I had seen over in England. But it was just superficial.

The depression started to overwhelm me again.

Eventually, the depression took over and I stopped working. For about six months, I didn't work, I didn't go out, I didn't do anything. At various points, doctors had suggested medication for the depression but I was terrified of that, my mother had such a bad time because of the valium that I was very frightened of any kind of medication, it wasn't an option. That was understandable perhaps, but the reality was that I was a 19-year-old girl with a very serious and deep depression, coping alone, unmedicated.

During those six months, I just stayed in the house, closed the curtains and literally didn't do anything. This was during the summer but I didn't enjoy any of the sunshine. I'd see people going up and down to the beach but I just wouldn't do anything. On a couple of occasions, I visited my sister otherwise I stayed in all the time. I did see another doctor who told me he believed that I needed medication urgently. I went along with him up to a point, however I was terrified of starting on medication. That's when I made a decision.

I wasn't going to collect the medication.

Eventually – to be honest I don't recall why or how – I went back to work. Soon after, I made friends with a girl called Marie who worked at the same store and lived close by, and quite quickly the depression started to lift. Marie and I did lots of things together, we would go to classes in the evenings, one of which was a dance and movement class, which awakened some memories in me of winning a Feis (an Irish music and singing competition) when I was seven. Her parents were lovely people and her dad adored his daughters. On some level I suppose I was once again attracted by the very things that were missing from my life. The happiness and security, of a loving family.

At the supermarket, the manager's name was Paul Heaslip and as it happened, he would be indirectly responsible for another huge shift in my life. A rival store opened up called The Cranford Centre in Stillorgan and my own manager got a job there. One day he asked me if I'd like to join him at the new place and I said yes.

I'd just taken a major decision in my life without even knowing it.

That new supermarket was owned by a family called Cosgrave. They had three daughters and four sons – one of the lads was a few years younger than me, a very tall and very kind young man by the name of Dermot.

I've been married to that supermarket owner's son for 33 years now.

CHAPTER 6

FINALLY, A PACK TO CALL MY OWN

From the first minute I met Dermot, we just got on famously. He used to deliver supplies to his father's supermarket. His brother Dave used to work there too and we all got on really well. I actually made great friends with Dave first. I enjoyed my job and was finding my feet a little bit more – although my depression yo-yo-ed a bit, it was nowhere near as bad as when I was stuck at home. For quite a while I had felt lighter in myself, and I hadn't been using anything – not food, not shopping and I was drinking much less – to cope. I'd begun to realise that this version of myself was the real me and I often thought, *Yes, Betty, this is you, let's get on with this!*

Dermot was only 18 and I was a few years older but the age gap was never a problem, we gradually started chatting more and more over the coming weeks and always had a lovely time. At first, he was so young he still had acne, was really lanky and had this long hair too and wore filthy jeans! After a few months, I said to his brother Dave, 'I'd love to have a night out with Dermot, there's something about him …' and Dave said 'He actually fancies you!'

Great!

Dave arranged for me and some friends to go to a pub in Terenure – without Dermot knowing, so as to surprise him – but on the actual night Dermot didn't fancy a drink and wanted to go to the pictures instead! So Dave explained what was happening and Dermot showed up at the pub to see me. We hit it off so well and spent the entire night in the pub chatting happily, then we went our separate ways; we met up again the next day and again chatted all night. Dermot didn't actually ask me out for about six weeks though – I was still with Steve.

After another night out with Dermot, I realised how much I liked him and so I broke it off with Steve. Dermot was still too nervous to ask me out but eventually he did and we started going out together. We started seeing each other regularly, it was really good but his parents were not happy because of the age gap and perhaps because I was from the wrong side of the tracks. In fact, initially they tried to actually stop the relationship. However, one day, his sister Emer said, 'Betty, he's changed so much since he's met you, he's dressing all differently, he's gorgeous. All my friends fancy him now!'

Eventually, I had to move jobs – I got on great with his father but the relationship with Dermot's mum was not so good. So, to make it easier for us, I went back to work at Quinnsworth. Dermot used to collect me every day for lunch and we'd go and have a bite to eat and a chat. Even then, his mum came into my work and asked me to leave her son alone, so it was very difficult at first. After a while, I said to Dermot, 'I think maybe you are very young and maybe your mum is right, let's finish this before it goes any further and we get hurt …' and I broke up with him. We'd been together about five or six months at this point and I'd moved in with a friend in Dundrum.

That very night, Dermot arrived outside my house. It was about two o'clock in the morning. He rang the bell but I wouldn't answer. He kept trying for a long time, walking up and down outside but eventually he gave up and trudged home. Then the next night he did the same again, up and down, up and down until finally I pushed the window open and shouted, 'Bloody hell Dermot! Come in will you!'

We held each other for a long time and both of us were crying, then I explained that I still wanted to see him but perhaps we should not tell his parents.

'No way, I'm not playing games Betty,' said Dermot. He's always been very straightforward and insisted that we had to just be together and for everyone to know. We were helped by the fact I got on with his sisters and brothers, they were thrilled I got with him.

A month later we got engaged!

Dermot is quite a spiritual person and although he does not perhaps use the same language as me in that way, we both knew we were soul mates. We both recognised we had a very deep soul connection, much deeper than just physical. We had a journey to go on together and we also knew that journey probably wasn't going to be easy. Exactly how difficult at times, neither of us could have imagined …

One of the very first things that Dermot had to get used to was my ability to see certain things before they happened. As I'd grown into adulthood, I'd realised that it wasn't just souls that I could see. I noticed that I also saw things before they actually occurred. At first, it took me a while to realise that it was happening more than once; then I mentioned it to a couple of friends and they just believed me without question.

Then a word of mouth started to spread locally and every now and then people would stop me in the street and say things like, 'Betty, I think I'm feeling a spirit in my house, would you help me clear it?' I'd go round their house and start seeing things, premonitions, whatever you wish to call it. It felt perfectly natural to me, just like talking to souls did, although I didn't even really know what I was plugged into at this stage.

I remember one day, I got a terrible feeling about the mother of one of my friends at work. Her name was Sharon. I told her that I had this feeling that her mother wasn't well and maybe she should give her a call. But before she had a chance to get to a phone, there was an announcement over the intercom, that there was a call for her. It was her brother calling to say that her mum had had some kind of attack, possibly a stroke and that she should go straight to the hospital.

Another time I had this vision about a girl called Sarah Jane, she worked in the chemist shop next door. I saw her up on a stage bowing and the audience was applauding. When I met her that day, I told her about my vision and she was surprised, because she had asked for time off to attend an audition, which was being held in the city but her employer had said no. I told her that she should just go because she wasn't going to need her job much longer. She did as I said and two weeks later, she was on a plane to New York. Sometimes, you've just got to trust!

One of the very first things I did after we got engaged was move back home. Even though I knew that was still not an ideal place to live, we desperately wanted to get married and the only way we would be able to save up for a nice wedding was for me to move back. This was not an ideal situation for me but we really didn't have any other option. Dermot wasn't being paid very well, due to the fact that his father's business had run into trouble, but I was, so I made that sacrifice.

We saved in the ICS building society branch in Dundrum and each week we got a little closer to having what we needed to pay for the wedding. Then disaster struck, there was a bank strike running up to the time of our big day and when we went into the branch to withdraw our money, we were told that they weren't in a position to give us all of our money. We were devastated and didn't know what we were going to do but luckily enough, the hotel was owned by a relative of Dermot's – Patrick Cosgrave – so we went up there the night before the wedding, to put out the place settings and explain our predicament. Even though they were related to Dermot, we didn't know how they would react but what happened was a revelation to us. We met Patrick's wife, Phyllis and she was so understanding and helpful, telling us not to worry, that we could pay whatever the balance was as soon as we could get it. Not only that, she instructed the chef to cook us a big steak dinner, with all the trimmings and then she sat with us and enjoyed a lovely meal. It meant so much to both of us.

On the morning of the wedding, my family were asking me not to go through with the wedding – members of both sides of the family thought it was unwise, for different reasons. Steve was a great guy and his family were invited to the wedding, but for us as a couple it wasn't to be. I wanted to be with Dermot. Steve went out with me at times when I was a very difficult girlfriend, he did not have it easy, as I have said. But Dermot gave me more stability – if he said he would turn up at a certain time, he would be there without fail.

So there we were, the wedding day arrived and my family went to the church leaving me to prepare by myself. I had to put my own wedding dress on. Even though I knew I was doing the right thing, the sense of abandonment was fiercely re-ignited. But there was *no way* I was going to let that spoil my big day. Dermot's Uncle Frank came in and saw I wasn't ready, so he went to get his wife, Joan, to help me get fully dressed. I always got on great with that couple and she kindly helped me get my dress right and put my veil on.

My brother Steve walked me up the aisle and it was a beautiful ceremony. All Dermot could see was me and all I could see was Dermot, we were *so* happy. Later, in the hotel, when Dermot's father stood up to give his speech, he said they hadn't really wanted me in the family at first, but now I was in and they'd accept me! Needless to say I was distraught. Nobody was really speaking up for me; no one was saying anything lovely about me, which was obviously hard so I got up and gave a lovely speech for myself. I said it didn't matter who said what, about acceptance, and that Dermot and I were so happy and at our 30th anniversary we'd all have a good laugh about our wedding day. Then another one of Dermot's uncles stood up and he said, 'Well, I've met Betty on many occasions now and I think she is wonderful and I think they are a wonderful couple ...' and it was all I could do not to jump up and shout 'YES!'

The stuff with my family was out front, people could see there was no electricity, people could see my mother was a gambler. With Dermot's family, his mother and father were business people, they all went to school, did their Leaving Certs, they all did conventional school, very different. But Dermot's mother wasn't very friendly towards me; she didn't like me, Dermot's dad used to sneak over and visit us, he once brought me these beautiful flowers and vase but he couldn't tell his wife that he would visit me. His sisters used to sneak over and visit me as well. Dermot's mother didn't really speak to me for a long time, she couldn't come to terms with me marrying Dermot at all. Even though she wouldn't see me and Kimmage was a good hour's walk to Churchtown, I was determined to make her accept me, so one day I walked over there and knocked on her door but she wouldn't let me in, no matter how long I knocked for. She just couldn't come to terms at first with Dermot being gone. She wasn't the first mother to feel that way, of course! And she won't be the last.

I thought Dermot's family was exactly what I wanted. Consciously from the age of four what I wanted was to belong to a pack. I thought this was going to be the thing with Dermot and his family but it wasn't always that easy. It was like an animal instinct in me. A pack. I just wanted to belong to something.

Instead of buying a house as newlyweds, we had a business, a little home bakery in Kimmage and we were living over it. They were magic times. It was very hard work but we were together and it was great. The previous bakery owner had someone stay back for a few weeks to teach Dermot the baking, as he'd never done it before. He picked it up really fast and before long he was doing all the baking and I'd serve in the shop. We'd be up very early in the morning at 4am to go to the markets for supplies, and the hours in the shop were very long too.

Back then, money wasn't plentiful, this was 1976 and the economic climate was very tough, the banks weren't giving out a lot of money and people were really struggling. We still had our weekends out though, when we'd go out and meet all our friends. We'd go to the rugby club or some clubs in town and then on the Sunday we'd have some rest (although on some Sundays we'd open the bakery!). We struggled financially, it wasn't easy to make money in the bakery trade, it was very hard work but we loved it!

It was such a lovely community around us, I loved it. We were there for a year when I became pregnant on Fran, our first born. While I was carrying him, I did suffer a few minor episodes and occasionally I'd have a panic attack, I was about to have a baby and bring someone into the world! Physically we were working extremely hard and I was suffering from low blood pressure so sometimes I'd just pass out literally behind the shop counter. There were a lot of customers and old people around and they'd just put a cushion from the chair under my head on the shop floor and start serving! It was lovely.

I was very excited finding out I was pregnant. I really was looking forward to it, I have to say. We had a very difficult birth with Fran, however; due to some internal physical problems I had previously been told that I couldn't have children in the normal way. The hospital knew there were complications with me before I went in, but they still had me go into labour for 36 hours before they decided to take action.

It was a very traumatic birth. Fran had a very, very difficult entry into this world and in fact the labour became so precarious that I had to have an emergency C-section anyway. After 36 hours of labour! Then because Fran had been distressed through the birth, his whole head was squashed; it was stretched unbelievably from front to back, it really compressed his face. Dermot nearly passed out when he first saw him and they wouldn't let me look at him for a couple of days.

Because the birth was so difficult, Fran was a very bad sleeper. For months we'd get no more than two hours a night. We had the business still but that wasn't doing very well and money was really tight, so adding the stresses of having a newborn to that made life very demanding. In fact, it got so bad that the only way we could get him to sleep was by putting him in his pram, lifting it into the back of our old VW van and driving around the streets. It was okay, as long as we kept moving but if we had to stop at a traffic light before he got to sleep, then he would just start screaming again. It really started to grind us down. We were very lucky at the bakery because the community rallied around us – sometimes when I could barely stand from exhaustion, one of our regulars would take Fran out in his little buggy just to give me five minutes rest. They were amazing people. But Fran just wouldn't sleep and it quickly started to get on top of us.

However, even though I was anxious about our circumstances, I knew we had to make it together as a couple. We had a job to do and that was to look after Fran, our baby. Dermot will back me up on this – I wasn't going to let this get the better of me and Dermot was certainly not going to be beaten either. So we sat down and I said, 'Look, we are going to have to do something about this, what can we do to make this easier? How can we find a solution for this?' We decided to take it in turns minding Fran through the night so that at least one of us was getting some sleep. Looking back, I think it's fair to say I was then – and still am – very good at stepping back and analysing what needs doing.

I don't fall down under things.

I never did – and never will – let anything beat me. I might be knocked down and down and down again, but I will always, always, *always* get back up and start again.

We loved Fran to bits and it wasn't his fault that he was a bad sleeper or that he'd had such a difficult birth. They'd told us at the birth that one repercussion might be hyperactivity and that was a handful to cope with, even though we knew why it was happening. Besides, we got so much pleasure out of him, we loved him to bits and he made us so, so happy.

You know now that my mother often showed more overt kindness to other children than her own. We were not a cuddly, tactile family in that way. So when Fran first arrived, even though I'd swore to myself that I would not be this way, initially I found it incredibly hard to cuddle him. I adored him with every bone in my body, but there was this barrier, this psychological hurdle that I faced.

There was simply no precedent in my family for that. We couldn't even sit next to my mother. There was very little conversation either. So when I had Fran and he'd want to cuddle up to me, I couldn't … and I felt so *guilty*. I was terrified that I was not bonding and yet when I looked down at him in his cot or lying on a sofa, I loved him *so* much. Dermot's family is far more conventional than mine and he was brilliant with Fran. He used to take him into the bakehouse and sing him songs and tell him stories; anything to keep him occupied and amused.

This continued for the first year of Fran's life. I'd be sitting on a chair and he'd come crawling up and climb next to me after a cuddle and I would literally freeze. But I knew I had to break the circle. I told myself it wasn't acceptable, it wasn't the right way to look after a child. *My* child.

I had to change. It was as simple as that, no matter how difficult it felt. From day one I knew this behaviour was wrong. But I refused to get involved in 'blame and shame' because that would get me nowhere – I might say here, for example, that I was like this because of what other people did to me, I didn't get enough love, that it was someone else's fault. That's no use to anyone. I have a choice, I am an adult and I have to make the choice to not let my child grow up in a cold and frozen environment. It is very empowering when you finally make that choice, because you alone can make that happen and when it does, it is fantastic. So eventually, I thought, *Betty you've got to change this now!*

So I went and got parenting classes and watched and listened. I also went to the local crèche to sit and be with the children, helping out for the morning. I just wanted to feel what it was like being closer to children. I really found it very challenging because I'd never had nice touches or hugs or even gentle conversation. In that aspect of my life, I was like a robot.

Gradually I felt my inner turmoil about this start to fade. I began holding Fran when he came over for a cuddle, then I'd start thinking about going over to him for a cuddle ... and before too long, I couldn't stop myself! It is the most beautiful and natural thing to do, to cuddle your child, it is a wonderful, wonderful experience and it is so simple and so easy.

Fran was a little ray of sunshine but away from the family, the business was really struggling and no matter how hard we worked, we couldn't get ahead. The banks were not lending any money, so we had little choice but to sell the bakery. Dermot decided to go into the milk delivery business with his uncle so we bought a milk float and he also started 'dressing' chickens (ie cleaning them out and preparing them for the barbeque!). This job was with a guy who had bought several of his father's shops when he had gone bankrupt. In fact Dermot ended up helping him run that business. No matter what Dermot puts his mind to, he does it, he's always been a very hard worker.

We bought a house in Tallaght after selling the bakery and then I became pregnant on Gerry. His birth was a completely different experience, it was also a C-section but it wasn't a long labour and he was a little doll who slept and ate really well. He was very easy to look after and was a very happy little man. At this stage Fran was two and a half and was also sleeping much better so that all helped. Fran loved Gerry, he absolutely loved having a little brother, he'd hold him and cuddle him all the time.

When Dermot was doing the milk we still had grave money worries. He was working *so* hard, I can't tell you. He was working two jobs to try to keep us afloat. Every morning Dermot would go for the milk at 3am and be home by maybe half six or seven for breakfast – I'd be up with the kids and breakfast all ready to see Daddy and the fire lighting, because he'd be going back out to another job shortly after. This had been going on for over a year, when one morning he began to feel ill on his delivery route. He went to his parents' house, as it was closest, but he only just made it. Once inside the door, he collapsed on the floor and lost consciousness. They brought him home to me at around 6 o'clock and I already had the lads up for breakfast. I had the fire lighting and Gerry was in his high chair eating a crust while Fran was bouncing around the room as usual. I remember Dermot's mother and father coming in with him; he was very ill and had basically had a breakdown. They brought Dermot in and said, 'You need to get him a doctor.' As it turned out, the doctor said he was suffering from complete exhaustion and it was all down to overwork and financial stress.

It's funny how you react when those around you are ill. Bearing in mind my own struggles to cope and keep my depression at bay, when Dermot had his breakdown I was very strong. I would not call myself a survivor now (because to be a survivor you have to be a victim) but back then I had to survive. So I gave him a lot of love and kept saying, 'We'll manage, Dermot, somehow we will be fine, you just get yourself better.' He was pretty much out of it for a few days but then he came back very quickly and very strong. He just really needed to rest, he was doing too many jobs and with two small children it was just too much.

Interestingly, Dermot's mother changed with me then. His father told me later that she couldn't believe I was up and about with the children, looking after them, getting them up for the day so well and so organised. Something changed in her, there was a little more respect there. I think she thought I stayed in bed all day or something. There was a little turn, she actually began to be nicer to me then.

Within a year, Dermot had sold his milk round and opened up a little video shop in Rathmines. This video shop proved to be a completely new and unexpected challenge for both of us. He opened a second store and also became involved in a photo-developing business, which unfortunately ended in failure and forced us to sell our home as part of a rescue package.

We closed down the new store and relocated the other one to a new unit and I opened a small store a few doors away, selling women's and baby clothes too, so we kept ourselves busy!

We were now in a rented house when I became pregnant on Adam, who is nearly seven years younger than Gerry. That was quite a big gap between the lads but it was never a problem. Adam was a great kid, gorgeous, I was chuffed with him, and the lads were as well. Finally I had *my pack*. I was so busy with life, I loved the lads and I loved being a mother.

Those years with the lads growing up were fantastic. We were under a huge amount of pressure financially but as a family it was wonderful times. The lads were brilliant. Fran was doing karate, winning trophies, riding BMX bikes, he was involved in lots of different sports. Gerry loved the football, if it wasn't football it was basketball, both the older ones loved sports. Our weekends were gone! We weren't having holidays at the time because we couldn't afford it, but they'd both go off to basketball camp, they were really happy kids together.

We had a lovely home life in Tallaght and the boys loved living on that estate. They went to a lovely school and were both doing very well, even though Fran had dyslexia. We actually had a special person working with him and he made great progress with her.

There was a black cloud waiting for us though.

Financial problems had come knocking again. The Revenue had registered a judgement against us and we had no way of paying. We couldn't even afford the rent on our home and had to give it up.

We thought we were doing grand and then all of a sudden it crashed in on us.

CHAPTER 7

A LOW POINT,
A TURNING POINT

We had absolutely no money and were still unable to pay rent on a home. A friend of mine who was very comfortable financially, allowed us to stay at a house he owned, without any rent for a year, to give us a chance to get back on our feet. At this time I could feel myself beginning to dip, so I often took myself off to the beach, to walk by the sea and think clearly about the next steps we would take.

I could see that the money trouble wasn't the biggest problem – it was the effect all of this was having on the children. We had moved to a totally new area, far away from the kids' friends; moving out of the school they loved and into a dreadful school near the new house. They joined halfway through the school year too which made it much harder for them to make new friends and settle in. We made a really very bad decision letting them go to that new school – I honestly think we'd have been better off keeping them at home for lessons. I'll be the first one to put my hands up, no doubt, about the lads and that school. Plus we couldn't afford Fran's extra schooling for dyslexia so that hit him hard too. Gerry was more easy-going, he is what I call my little 'floating spirit'. Despite the fact he was bright, the new school affected his progress badly. In my opinion, that school actually wrecked their learning. It was devastating to me when I realised how badly it affected them both. The bad school … that nearly killed me, there was nowhere else to put them … I felt like everything was collapsing around me. Even so, I was still coping very well and we were now sitting down and trying to look towards the future.

Because the education the two lads had been receiving was totally inadequate, the whole school thing was a trouble for them. Fran is very like me, he doesn't suffer fools gladly. In school when the teachers were rude, he'd say, 'Don't speak to me like that', he just wouldn't stand for them being plain rude. Obviously this didn't make him many friends among the teachers! Unfortunately, Fran was also bullied quite a bit at that school and he found it much more difficult to make friends than Gerry. Fran was always his own man, he dressed differently, he was always outrageous, he was an out-going kid by nature. But while he was being bullied, he became introverted for a while, he withdrew quite a lot, until eventually he decided to make a stand. After that he never looked back!

Our financial troubles had been in the papers so people were after us for bad debts and the banks were chasing us for money too. It was just awful. Bear in mind we had two young boys and a baby under one year old. I sat down with Dermot one night and said, 'We are really in trouble here, we need to change certainly one part of our lifestyle straight away.' We still enjoyed having a good night out and a few drinks, but it seemed that we weren't going to get anywhere until we started accumulating some money. I decided that if I wanted to get back on track, then the obvious thing to do was give up alcohol and keep a clear head. Dermot agreed with me and so we both decided to do it together. A united front, if you like. When I look back though, I'm proud that we both had the clarity of mind as well as the conviction to stop the drinking. We took responsibility for our own situation and made a change.

Unfortunately, although we made great strides and our finances improved, my depression reared its ugly head once more, it was suffocating me. There was so much to deal with, to think of, to make decisions about.

I got very ill.

It all just became too much for me.

I switched off again, except this time, unlike when I was a child, I couldn't seem to find my way back. I began to notice that I would be still in my dressing gown at one o'clock in the day and I would find it very hard just to get myself going. For a long number of months, I found it difficult to leave the house.

Quite often, when I opened the hall door I would pass out. All these really horrific smells were coming back.

I had overloaded, so my mind and body switched off.

Shut down.

Occasionally I would blank out completely. At the time, however, things were different for us; I'd have an episode and blank out without warning. Dermot knew what to do – he and the lads knew how to react. For the next half hour or so, they'd just step over me and say, 'Ah, Mam will be back in a few minutes.' It sounds almost comical, but that was their way of coping in the circumstances they found themselves in. It's not something I'd necessarily recommend!

I was so ill they sent me to a psychologist as an urgent referral. She spoke with me and analysed what I'd said and done, then compiled a report that spoke about my symptoms, my circumstances and my prospects for recovery and the future.

What that report said could have potentially ruined the rest of my life.

The report was horrifying. It was truly harrowing reading.

At the time, in among all the problems we were having, its impact was far, far worse. The psychologist said that I was far below average intelligence and shouldn't waste my time thinking about education because ultimately I would fail, which would have dire consequences for my mental state. Further, she questioned my ability to be a proper parent to my children. Sitting there listening to those words after everything that I had gone through was deeply devastating and very disturbing …

… and yet … and yet … when I read them over and over again and in my mind – this battered, troubled mind – I kept saying to myself …

THIS IS NOT ME!

I knew the words on the page stated certain facts about my lifestyle that were true. I did suffer from depression. In parts when it detailed what I'd lived through, I remember thinking, *How the hell am I still on this planet?* It mirrored a lot back to me. But it was all so destructive. But that was her clinical opinion of what she saw that day when she met me. But leading up to that meeting, I'd collapsed into a mental minefield and this wasn't how I was always going to be. We'd got all those money worries. I was very troubled by the boys going to the horrible school. This was not the usual Betty Cosgrave.

And it was most certainly not the future Betty Cosgrave.

There was no way I wasn't a good mother. I was a great mother and I knew I could go on to be even better.

The picture she painted, had such dreadful implications for me, that I could find only one response: NO WAY, THAT IS NOT GOING TO HAPPEN.

Having listened as she described her view of my circumstances, I went home and sat down with Dermot to read it again and he was horrified too. Looking back, and given that I was cracking up because the house of cards was falling in on me, I'm not really sure how that report was supposed to help.

I remember us talking and I was convinced – as ill as I was – that I would never be this ill again, never mind be written off like that. 'There's no way this is me, Dermot,' I said. 'There are ways and means of me learning from this. Okay, I've had a lot of trauma in my life and this is just another trauma, these past few months have almost killed me and it certainly has traumatised me but *I am not done yet*.'

Between us we determined that this was not going to ruin me, I would not have that report end my life. *Our* life.

That week of the psychologist's report was actually the last time I got that ill.

I knew I had to totally look again at every aspect of my life: what I was eating, what I was thinking, exercise …

I also knew I needed more skills than that to get on in life – so I went and spoke to Father Paul Andrews, a local priest who used to work with wayward teenagers, a very kind man. He encouraged me to improve on my reading and writing problems. It made a lot of sense, because then I could start to read books and open up a whole new world to myself. I'd been helping Dermot run the business, speaking with bank managers and all, with no ability to read or write. Father Paul helped me enrol at the VEC in Bray which was a government scheme set up for people to attend a college who had not been schooled or were below average skills in terms of writing and reading. It's all free and voluntary – I went there for six months initially working one on one, learning basic spelling and reading skills with this really helpful lady. Back at home Dermot helped my hugely. He'd sit down with me for hours getting through homework.

After six months I was able to join a group and after that I never looked back. I'd got my basic reading and writing skills so now I could feed my taste for learning … and my appetite was literally insatiable.

Once that was under my belt, the world really was my oyster.

I could read any book in the world so I could think about any concept in the world.

Suddenly, there was no limit.

No matter what the psychologist's report said, I knew I had a great connection with my children and that I was a good mother. I believed I was a very good, supportive wife and a very good businesswoman. I was a good person.

I just *had* to take charge.

And that's exactly what I did.

CHAPTER 8

A NEW PATH

I began training as a Reflexologist. Reflexology is the treatment of physical symptoms by working on points on the feet, which correspond with the various organs in the body. It can bring balance and harmony to the body, mind and spirit. Why? Well, I was very attracted to the idea of helping other people. Training as a Reflexologist was a way of starting to help people without interfering with my other gifts. I read up about it and found it very interesting, so I enrolled on a training course.

It was a twelve month diploma course in Reflexology and while this was very challenging for me, I was determined to succeed. Shortly after I began, I met a Reflexologist who became aware of my circumstances and offered me her support. She was amazingly patient with me on the written work. I found the practical side of the discipline very natural, but the written theory was more of a struggle. While I was doing all this training, I realised that my self-esteem, my self-worth was very low. Some of my relationships within my wider family seemed to reaffirm that I was 'no good'.

But as each day passed, my self-worth grew.

I began to see – *really see and believe* – that I *was* a good mother, a good wife, a good woman. I remember when I passed my Reflexology exam, Dermot's father told me that he knew I loved Dermot and that I was a great mother, and he was so proud of me for passing my exams – the delight in him for me … he wanted to come and watch me get my diploma even though that's not allowed! That was wonderful for me and very kind of him.

All of a sudden, I started owning the real me.

My soul self.

After the Reflexology course, I heard about Reiki and Kinesiology, my mind was swirling with all these amazing new thoughts, concepts and ideas. Then I found out about Neuro-linguistic Programming, otherwise known as NLP. I started buying books on that subject and all sorts of other ideas and theories, then I found audio CDs and that was even more helpful.

I *devoured* them all.

I'll introduce you to a few of these ideas later, but for now, all I need to tell you is that these and other ideas were like the most delicious *food* for my brain. Maybe when I had shut down and become so ill, my brain and mind had simply needed to regenerate. I don't know, maybe it was just a symptom of being very ill. What I do know is that after all those years of not being able to read and write and being so limited, I was like a butterfly opening its wings.

This was a time when Dermot and I were very close, I have to be honest and say that was probably the best few years of our whole marriage for me. Eventually the video shops were doing much better and gradually we began to get back on our feet. So *finally* we had some daylight …

Dermot obviously knew about my gifts, it was no surprise to him. Besides, we'd periodically experience something that he knew was a direct result of what I could see. So for example, after we'd agreed a repayment plan with the banks and just started to get ourselves back on our feet, I said to him one day, 'Dermot, we are going to see somebody walking in off the street and they are going to offer us IR£54,000 to buy one of our shops. We will then have the money to put a small deposit on a house. I see it.'

A week later, a friend of Dermot's got in touch to say that he knew someone who wanted to buy a video store so we met him and agreed a price of IR£81,000 but the strange thing was that after we paid off what we owed the bank etc., we had IR£54,000 left over.

We cleared our remaining debts, put a deposit down on a house and we were back on the pig's back.

We had an amazing seven years after that.

We bought the new house and it needed an awful lot of work doing to it. Nobody had lived there for fifteen years and it was a bit of a wreck. There were about 100 families of rats under the floors and in the gardens so when we moved in, the vermin started running out into the streets – all the neighbours were horrified! Eventually we had to get the council out to get rid of all the rats properly.

The house was looking over open farmland out the back and there were beautiful horses to look at. We gutted the kitchen straight away, put in a new staircase and beautiful floors, it was gorgeous, then we decided to work on the rest of the house over a longer period of time.

I didn't care, I had a house – a home – again.

I bought a plinth and put it in the front room and started taking clients for Reflexology. Within a short while, I was booked up two months in advance. People would say, 'I don't know what you did but I've had bad sinuses for years and now I can breathe again.' Sometimes the treatments would be straight-forward but other times I'd sense something unusual going on, perhaps see something that was about to happen in the future or maybe even see a soul in the room while I was working on the person, and that would lead the session in another direction altogether. Very naturally and very quickly, my clinical and theoretical practices became a vessel for my ... how shall I say ... 'less conventional' gifts to present themselves. I knew that the gifts I had – the ability to see souls and events before they happened – were something very precious. But I never charged for my gift and I never offered it as a service. People often ask me why I didn't set up charging money for contacting souls and seeing things. Sometimes people will ring me up and say, 'I want a reading please.' I always say 'I don't do readings, sorry.' I am very firm about that. I don't have that access. That was never an option, *never*. It would not cross my mind. What I have is a gift and it certainly was not something that I could send out and charge for, that's totally against my position.

Word of mouth spread very quickly and it wasn't long before I had as much work as I could cope with.

With the lads, we were both conscious of rebuilding their confidence from all the knocks at school, so one day we sat down with them and suggested a family project – we would build our very own basketball court. The lads jumped at the idea and so, the very next day they started digging a big hole in the garden and they just kept digging and digging until they'd basically cut out a basketball court!

We got a quarry to deliver two lorry loads of gravel for the foundation and soon after that we had a cement firm come and pump the cement right over our house straight into the foundation and they had the most amazing basketball court in the back garden. It was back-breaking work for them but it was really bonding too and they got years of enjoyment from it.

As a family we never let all the problems trouble us. We were always doing something! We got them skateboards too and other kids would come over and play on those. We did loads of things, went to the park at weekends, skateboarding as a family, basketball, we stayed good *together*.

Although I don't practice Reflexology now, it was a starting point for me. I kept training in new skills at every opportunity. I got so fascinated by learning that I sat down with Dermot and the lads and said, 'I am so excited, I want to train with the best and I might have to be gone for a weekend every now and then, okay.' I wanted them to be aware of what I was doing and why. They were great about it and pleased that I had something so fulfilling. When I sometimes wondered if I had the brain capacity to cope with this mass of new information, Dermot said without a moment's hesitation, 'Of course you do! I'll have the lads.' For the next three years I was constantly on courses, reading books, attending seminars, learning, learning, learning …

… and that was the path that has brought me out of Wolfe Tone Square, out of my mental abyss, away from escapism, from compulsive thoughts, from insecurity … into a happy and contented life. It's a path that started at the little gate by the unkempt garden outside my house, led me up the hill where I used to hold hands with that beautiful arthritic lady, Kate, off through all sorts of challenges with my 'pack' and finally into a world of learning that has no boundaries. It is

the path that has taught me many wonderful skills and ideas
– some of which I'd now like to share with you – and has
eventually drawn me to be sitting here writing this book,
talking to you.

I'm grand.

PART II

THE
WHISPERING
SOUL

CHAPTER 9

ALL PART OF A BIGGER PICTURE

I do not see myself as a ghost-whisperer. See, I don't call them ghosts. I call them spirits. I'm very uncomfortable with the word ghost although I don't know why. It's obviously something inside myself because anytime I do have an experience, to me they are just spirits who have unfinished business here.

Likewise I don't do readings. I cannot just call up spirits. I am not a psychic or a medium. Seeing souls is not something I can control in that way. I must say though, that I am not cynical of people who call themselves ghost-whisperers. Some people genuinely do have a gift. In my opinion, that is a simple fact. There absolutely are genuine people. There are also, of course, some people who are not genuine and I can see it may be difficult for most members of the public to tell the difference. But I am telling you there are genuinely gifted people out there. I do believe there are people who have that ability but I am not one of them.

So let me give you an example of how a soul will come to me personally. I had a girl who periodically used to come to me for healing when she was stressed. I hadn't seen her for many months but even so, when people come to me for healing, we don't chat away for half an hour before I start. We say hello for a couple of minutes then I get them up on the bed, which is exactly what I did on this particular day.

Initially, they will stay quiet and I get them into a state of relaxation. However, after only a few minutes something happened.

'Rita, has your mother passed away since we last spoke?'

'Yes, Betty,' she said. 'I thought you knew. Anyway, there's a lot of trouble in the family since and it's been really hard and stressful.'

'With your sister and brother?'

'Yes. How did you find out?'

I could see Rita's late mother standing in an apron at the end of the bed. Unlike when I was a little girl in the graveyard, however, I don't always speak out loud and in this case I just heard her mother's thoughts.

'Rita, you know what I do. Do you wish me to continue?'

I always ask if they wish me to explain or not, it's essential to have that approval. I am very careful how I deliver, I am very careful how I communicate. I do it with such integrity and from the heart and when we do it from the heart and soul it's for everyone's highest good. So I will always say something like, 'Take it or leave it, if it makes sense to you great, if it's going to facilitate you to make your soul more content and be happy on the planet, take it and use it; if you don't understand it, feel free to dismiss it.'

Rita wanted me to continue.

'Well, your mum is here right now,' I said. 'She's wearing an apron, a little pink one with teddies on it.'

'Betty, she died in that apron.'

Her mother's soul had worn the apron to verify what I was saying. I could not have known that detail so her mum wore that as a signal to Rita that I could see her.

Rita said that she and her sister had 'felt' their mother in the kitchen of the family home. This showed me that they were both naturally inclined to tune in, but they just hadn't been able to pick it up fully.

'Well, your mum cannot pass over until this is resolved, Rita,' I explained. 'She tells me that her children are her life's work and she cannot have it end up like this. She's asking can you all meet up in the house, all arrive at the same time, that's very important, no one is to arrive first. She will give some signal to you that she is there. She needs you to organise a family meeting. This has to be resolved. She never meant her Will to actually offend any member of the family. Do you understand, Rita?'

She did. Perfectly.

It transpired that one of Rita's sisters didn't have a home of her own so her mother had left more to that sister than the other siblings, in order that she wouldn't have to worry about trying to buy a home. But the brother in particular wasn't happy and had stopped speaking to the rest of the family, he was very angry. It was tearing the family apart. And, as I now knew, it was doing the same to the mother.

'But how will I know her signal?' asked Rita.

At this point, I asked her to quieten her mind. Sometimes at this point, the actual person may pick up on the soul's presence, it is not impossible. I asked her to do deep breathing and relax, listen to her heart beat.

Rita and her sister had already felt a sense of their mother being there, but it wasn't until I asked her to quieten her mind that she actually paid proper attention to that.

Then, suddenly, Rita said …

'Scones with nutmeg. That will be the signal.'

The family had the meeting at the house, in the kitchen in fact. They talked about the tensions and the problems were resolved.

Rita's mother was able to pass over.

And I don't need to tell you about the beautiful baking smell they all noticed in the kitchen as they talked.

So how do I explain 'souls'? What do I actually mean when I say 'soul'?

Well, in my opinion, there are several levels to any person. On the surface, there is what is known in some schools of thought as the 'programming'. This is the part of you that is shaped by society, by school, by work and by the establishment. Parents, teachers, peer groups, they are all part of your programming. Some of those programmes really help and are very positive for people, but at the same time they are actually going away from a vital aspect of your life. In simple terms, you might say that young children have a beautiful 'innocence' about them. Part of that is because they are not yet in the system, they haven't gone to school and become part of that structure. Once we enter the 'system' that is society, a lot of sensory attunement is often lost. Children have this sense more than adults until they go into school. You know when children set their place for their imaginary friend? … it's their angel, or guide. It's for a soul. Parents can't see that because programming has taken them away from that sense.

The next level is beneath your programming – your DNA. This is your body. Remember Edie? My beautiful aunt. I mentioned her DNA was responsible for her stunning looks and elegant presence. Likewise, your own attributes are due to your DNA. This DNA can be responsible for some of the patterns we display in our life.

Yet even further inside is our essence, our core self, our *soul*. I honestly believe that we have an essence – our soul self – within ourselves that we need to resonate with. Stripping back all these layers and listening to that soul is vital to your well-being ... but we'll come to that in a moment.

Before we look at our own soul self – the most intimate and precious thing you will ever possess – let's take a step back and look at the bigger picture. You may or may not believe in God. I don't know, that's a deeply personal issue and entirely up to you. I don't believe in the God my father taught me, I dismissed him at the age of three when I was standing in Mass and my father was ranting that everyone's troubles were caused by me. That version of God has nothing to do with me. The God of my understanding is a forgiving God and a loving God.

I am not talking about the God of any religion, I'm talking about something that's bigger than myself, bigger than us, a higher being. Numerous religions would call it their God; other people would be less orthodox and call it Mother Nature; or maybe someone else would call it 'something out there'. Call it whatever you wish. I believe that there *is* something bigger than us and that we are all connected to it. Some of us are more attuned than others and this explains why some people have a gift and some people don't. It explains why some people seem more at ease with themselves and others appear to be always struggling.

I'm not the first person to suggest this, of course, there have been many eminent thinkers and writers who have discussed this before. There are lots of different theories about this and it makes for fascinating reading! Dr David Hawkins wrote about his theory that we are all connected to an energy field and this is his version of the higher being. I'll give you a more mundane example. Have you ever thought of someone, maybe decided to phone them or text them soon, and then the phone rings and it is that very person?

That's because you are both tuned into the magnetic field and the thoughts were passing back and forth. It's coincidence some might say! That's their view, not a bother. I feel that is not a coincidence. Also, the closer you are with someone, the more likely this is to happen. It's like tuning into a radio, just tuning into the collective consciousness. Some people might hear, some might see, some might get a sense. It's not logical, there is no logic to it, it's beyond our five senses, it's beyond consciousness.

Let me give you another example directly from one of my sessions. I have a gentleman called James who comes to see me on occasion. He's very 'left-brain' – the considered, rational side – a man with a very logical way of looking at things. He came to me and said, 'I know you do Reiki, because my friend sees you, but he also says it's more than just Reiki although he couldn't explain why. I have this anxiety inside me and I can't get rid of it. I have tried all sorts of treatments but it's not moving and it's really affecting my day-to-day life.'

Reiki is a form of hands-on healing and it is a practice I use very often with my clients – that and other types of hands-on and absent healing. I think everyone has the healing ability. What I am is a channel for healing. All I am is a channel. People who come to me for Reiki or hands-on healing report feeling a lot of heat in their body when I work on them, they feel tingling going on in their bodies, they may even see colours. I don't call myself a healer – what I am doing is tuning them into their own healing ability with what I do. Everybody heals themselves, everyone has the ability within themselves to tune into it.

I put James up on the plinth and I started to tune into his energy. When I talk about 'energy' here, I mean his soul.

'James, I could be right or wrong but there is something

and it's important for me to throw this out to you, you can take it or leave it.'

'That is why I am here, Betty. What is it?'

'Your father is here. I know he's not dead but I know he's very ill and I know you haven't spoken about him but it seems to be very important. If you want me to stop I certainly will, just say so … but it seems to be important. He is telling me something which might sound a bit crazy but I'm just going to come right out and tell you anyway and if you think I'm crazy that's okay, ignore it.'

'I'm fine, Betty, please continue,' said James.

'Your father says he wants you to forgive the birds.'

James just burst out crying uncontrollably right there on the plinth.

The man shook the bed with his crying, he cried and cried, loudly and emotionally.

When he finally stopped, he seemed already calmer, so I was hopeful I had helped.

'Betty, I have had those tears in me since I was seven years old. My father is very ill and we haven't spoken for 25 years. When I was a kid, he kept pigeons and I always felt those pigeons meant more to him than I did. In fact, on one occasion he actually said that. For so many key points of my life he wasn't there because of those pigeons. I hated those birds.'

James resolved to go and see his father a week later.

Why did that happen?

My view is this: James and his father were connected into the same energy field. I tuned into his father and simply connected them both together. His father would have been thinking of James, of his pigeons and of the tension at the same time – somewhere else in the world – as James was lying on my plinth and I made the connection for them.

You may have your own opinion. That is mine.

A wonderful off-shoot of tuning in like this is the ability to scan a person's body and get information. When James lay on my plinth I tuned in to his soul but at the same time I was scanning his body, and I could tell exactly where this tight ball of anxiety was that was causing him so many problems. In extreme cases, I can tell that people have health problems with specific organs in their body just by scanning them – I can literally see the physical organ and the illness very clearly; I can also sometimes tell if a person is allergic to certain things using the same process.

Scanning like this involves me in what is another level of a person – their blueprint. In my opinion, we all come in with blueprint. You know those lovely pieces of very old wood you can buy which come with a certificate telling you the year and age the scientists think this tree started to grow? Those slices of wood tell the scientists an awful lot of information about what has happened to that tree; well, a blueprint is exactly the same only it can tell me an awful lot about what will happen to someone in the future. I can read your blueprint just as methodically as the scientists read those slices of wood.

I believe we all come in with a journey and that there is something special for us to do in this lifetime – most of the time I can actually see that journey with people's blueprints. When I meet someone, I can often read their blueprint within seconds of shaking their hand, it can be that fast. Over the years, I have found this to be very helpful with clients who need detailed work, because reading their blueprint can often help me leapfrog over weeks of meetings to get straight to the very heart of the problem.

I am not suggesting that we all have a pre-destined fate and there is nothing we can do to alter that. For example, our lifestyle will heavily affect our journey. I might see someone's blueprint as having them live to a ripe old age, but if that adult chooses to drink excessively, smoke 40 a day and take very little care of their body, then that clearly may affect their blueprint. So it's not set in stone. But reading someone's blueprint, like James's when I scanned him, is a really helpful benefit of being able to tune in.

I am obviously aware that some people are cynical of this idea of an energy field, of tuning in, of blueprints and so on. I know that people may well attribute these 'coincidences' or experiences to something else, all of that doesn't really matter at all. The fact is, in my opinion, we are on this planet and are all part-connected with this planet and with each other. I know that since I was a child, I have been plugged into *something*, there is no doubt in my mind. That is where the information I hear and see comes from. I have been fine-tuning that ability since I was a little girl.

Now, don't get me wrong, I don't go round tuned in all the time. I go out for meals and shopping and seeing my grandson and I live my life and enjoy it and maybe don't see or hear anything for ages. These experiences generally happen when I am working or when I am in meditation for myself, when I am tuning in either for a client or because I want to learn something for myself. Sometimes if I am thinking as I walk along a street, it will happen, but usually it is when I am meditating or working. When I feel it happening, I allow myself to be open to any information that needs to come in. It's also completely random, sometimes it will happen three times in one day then I'll get nothing for a week. I've noticed more recently that when I am working it can happen mostly all the time. I think the fine-tuning is getting sharper and sharper, you never stop learning and fine-tuning.

An interesting point from my personal experience is that this tuning in has never been a negative aspect of my life. There have never been times when I've been traumatised by what's come to me. I think it's because these situations are not my responsibility, other people are involved and in fact all I am doing is trying to help, to resolve, to make things better. Obviously I prefer it when matters are resolved but it's always been a wonderful thing for me, never a negative.

'So why', you might ask, 'is Betty tuned in but I'm not?' Well, in my experience, we all have the potential to tune in. We can all do it. Some people are tuned in naturally, some have to work at it and still others will probably never tune in, probably due to a variety of reasons. However, many people I speak to tell me of experiences they have had that they can't necessarily explain logically. Some of these people are very left-brain thinkers, professionals, lawyers, accountants, in one case an eminent Neuroscientist – he told me that there are fundamental things the brain does that even the most advanced science cannot explain. For example, no one actually knows how the brain produces that human experience we call 'consciousness'. Therefore, it follows that if you know there are limitations about your knowledge of the brain, then how can you say with certainty that it definitely cannot do certain things. That in itself is not a logical position to take: *I absolutely don't know everything the brain does, but I'm 100% sure it doesn't do these things.*

People are very surprised when I tell them this – if someone as academically talented and scientifically qualified as this Neuroscientist can consider that individuals have a potential that we as humans are not yet fully aware of clinically, then it convinces me that there are things going on out there, that we cannot explain and that we are all, in theory, capable of tuning into. In fact, I believe you can train yourself to tune in, should you wish to.

Let me give you a more specific example. One of my friends asked me about an experience he'd had while on holiday in Cornwall. He'd visited a famous coaching inn that was renowned for reports of ghosts. Personally he was not particularly a firm believer one way or the other at that point: he neither dismissed nor championed the idea. He was staying there for a night with his beautiful wife and small baby boy.

During the night, the man awoke to see the curtain in the room blowing gently right next to where his baby was asleep in a cot. Thinking nothing of it, he went back to sleep. Then some time later, he was lying facing the edge of the bed when he felt his wife's hand on his forehead, mopping it as if taking his temperature. His eyes were shut but he smiled at her gentle touch and said, 'It's alright, I'm not ill, I feel fine ...'

At that point, he opened his eyes and saw that his wife actually had her back to him and was fast asleep. It couldn't have been her hand.

He came to me and asked me what had happened that night. To me it was obvious. He'd tuned into a spirit. Maybe a lady had cared for sick travellers in another life and had some unfinished business, or maybe she felt she'd let someone down and not looked after them properly. I didn't know the exact reason for that soul to visit him, what I did know was that he had tuned into a spirit.

Other people may have felt or experienced something similar, but never put it into words or articulated it to anyone else. They may be a bit nervous simply because there can be a lot of fear and cynicism around such matters and people don't want to feel 'silly'.

All I would say to you is this: we all have the ability to tune in but it's up to you whether you choose to.

So having read that these souls are there and we can tune into them, you might ask next, 'But why are they there at all?'

Well, if you recall what those souls told me when I was a five-year-old girl in the graveyard ... that if someone has no unfinished business, they will pass over within three days. If there are issues still to be resolved, they may not pass over so quickly; if there are more serious problems, then it may take a longer time for this to happen. I say they are floating between this world and another, wherever they should be heading. Hopefully the issues can eventually be resolved and those souls can rest and pass over.

When I say 'pass over', what do I mean? My view is that they reconnect with the magnetic energy field, with the higher being or whatever you wish to call it – 'back into the light' some people call it.

But what happens after they have passed over? The soul goes on to the next journey. In my opinion, souls have the choice. Some will just pass over and go into the spirit world; others choose to come back as angels and guides, to watch over their loved ones left behind and see the lives that are being lived; other souls become guides for troubled souls; still others choose to come back into another person. In other words, some souls choose to reincarnate.

Many souls will come back. I came into this planet with a consciousness. I absolutely believe in reincarnation. I believe when the soul leaves the body – this physical body – to go to the next journey, that it carries with it the consciousness of things it has already learned.

But not every soul reincarnates endlessly. Each time a soul goes through the journey of life, they are learning, achieving a higher spiritual consciousness, learning lessons each time around. Constantly evolving. Each reincarnation is to bring us into a higher spiritual reality.

This is why you might sometimes come across a little lad of six years old or so, saying things that seem unduly wise, 'an old head on young shoulders' as they say. It's because he's been here before.

Or, remember your friend who always seems to text or

phone you at the exact moment you were thinking of them? I know I've explained about you both being connected to something bigger than us, but when this happens a lot, when it is more frequent than other friends, I believe this is because you will have had past life connections with that person.

I also believe that there is such a thing as cellular memory – by this it is meant that your cells have memories of previous and current life experiences. Your body has a memory deep in its cells. I believe this memory is carried from one life to the next, in the essence of ourselves, in our authentic selves, the soul, when we reincarnate. It doesn't make any other sense to me as to how I was able to see souls at such a young age. I couldn't have had it in me any other way at that age other than through cellular memory. This memory is in the soul.

I am not alone in this thinking. There have been various studies made into this phenomenon and there was actually an article published in one particular alternative therapy journal that included anecdotal evidence that some organ donor recipients had experienced changes in their personality, tastes and ideas after receiving someone else's body parts (this included suddenly loving classical music for example or acquiring a taste for strong cheese when previously it had been disliked).

You may feel reincarnation is something you don't believe in – and I am very aware that many people will disagree with me on this, that not everyone shares my opinion here. I don't argue for it, everybody has their own reality, and their own reality is their fact. If someone is just totally left-brained, it means that they may have shut the unconscious, the soul part of themselves, into a compartment or they just may not be connected with it at all. Their journey may be just totally of *this* world. All I know is just my perception and my reality, these are my experiences. Likewise, I would never dismiss someone else's views and say something is or something isn't the case, because I believe every human being on this planet has their own journey, their own belief system and their own programming and they are entitled to that.

So, here you have my view on souls, on why they speak with me, why they may or may not speak with other people and why certain things happen in life that we can't explain.

That's all part of a bigger picture. It's time to shrink it all down to a personal level.

To you.

What part do souls play in someone's life?

What part does *your* soul play in *your* life?

CHAPTER 10

THE WHISPERING SOUL

When I take a moment to quieten myself and feed my spirit, something very special happens. This is when I can hear my soul whispering to me. What do I mean by that? Let me tell you.

A lot of people get so tied up in day-to-day life and all the rushing about and stress that this involves. It is so easily done. However, *it is absolutely essential to keep your spiritual self well.* This is separate from your mental, physical and emotional self. What I am talking about is the spiritual self – now that can mean different things to different people but for me, I believe that what carries us through the really traumatic times is our spiritual beliefs, whether that's a God or a universal energy, whether it's nature, or whatever.

I call it the soul, some may call it the core self or the authentic self. This is the core self without all the programming. You need to pull back from the programming when you are doing this and only listen to the core self, your soul.

The point is, we have to take time out *each day* to feed the spiritual self. This is crucial for your well-being. *Crucial.*

The simplest way of doing this is to go for a walk. This isn't rocket science here, but if you go for a fifteen-minute walk, maybe half an hour, then you are at least giving yourself the opportunity to listen to yourself. *Oh, but my job's too busy for that!* I hear you say. Well, try doing this first thing in the morning. *Yes, but I'm always in a rush getting out of the house!* Well, maybe get up just fifteen minutes earlier. If you can't do this because of time or maybe children or a long commute, how about during the lunch break, take a stroll for a sandwich from a shop a little further away? Or is it possible to get a slightly earlier train in and have ten minutes quiet in the office before it all goes crazy? It's not a long time we are talking about here.

So how do you listen in to your Whispering Soul?

Firstly, you need to quieten the mind. If you can't hear yourself think – or sometimes even talk – because of all the noise and chaos around you, then how can you possibly listen to the whispering of your soul? So shut out physical distraction and then quieten your mind. If the mind is working, it is hard to get in touch with the heart and the soul.

I just say to myself, *I have no mind*, and with that it's like pressing the Delete button on a computer and the left logical brain just goes quiet. Then I do nice deep breathing, in through the nose, out through the mouth. Any thoughts that might float in I pay them no attention and just let them float away. Then I pay specific attention to the heart and listen closely to the heart beat itself. I am connecting with my heart and focusing in on it. If you get this right you may even be able to feel the flow of blood going through your heart. Tell yourself, *No thoughts, quiet mind, thoughts are leaving me, quiet mind*.

Pay attention to your breathing. Breathe in through the nose and hold for the count of four, and breathe out through the nostrils for the count of four. If you simply do this three or four times, then that alone will start to quieten your mind.

If I'm lucky and able to do so, I go to walk by the beach and sit and open up my arms and take in the energy, the sea holds amazing energy and has a resonance, the rhythm of the sound of the sea never changes, that sound automatically and totally clears my mind so that all I hear is the sound of the sea. Again that may not work for you. Maybe meditation will be an option? Or simply that little walk. Only you can know what works best.

If you recall that little five-year-old girl rocking back and forth in silence in that dingy sitting-room in Ledwidge Crescent, I would go blank and quiet, go inwards. When I look back, I can see now what I was doing. I was listening to my soul. I was having that conversation. The establishment may have looked at that and said I was a girl in need of help, but to my mind, I had taken the quiet time to listen to my essence. Of course, I didn't know it was meditation back then, I didn't call it meditation until much later in life. But that's what it was. I would shut out all the physical and emotional noise and clutter of my little life and get back to my soul. A soul I had done everything in my power to protect. And now it was rewarding me by gently whispering.

Don't be put off by my use of the word 'meditation'. It may not be sitting for half an hour with your legs crossed – that certainly doesn't suit me or work for me! – but maybe going for a walk, maybe thinking of nothing except nature, maybe watching a bird flying and concentrating on the bird, or maybe there's a little breeze and you hear a little rustle of the leaves, that's all meditation, that's getting in touch with your spirit self, your soul.

If you have a mantra that works for you, then repeat it gently. Some of the schools of thought I am trained in use mantras and for many people these are very, very powerful. It resonates with them. Or maybe there's a prayer that resonates with you. However, keep it simple. Reciting a complex prayer for example may make you stumble over the words and when that happens, your left logical brain kicks in and then that will drown out your soul. There'll be a battle of wills going on. Simplicity is the key.

These are all just suggestions – you will find your own way of doing this. It gets easier, even though being distracted is all too easy at first. If someone says 'Don't think of a pink elephant' then that instinctive reaction and thought – you've probably just done it yourself! – takes time to avoid. And know this – the more you practice listening to your soul, the easier it becomes. Over the years, I've become quite adept at listening to my soul and so I will often just sit in a quiet room and listen in, as simple as that. Quite soon it will come very naturally to you too and you will look forward to those moments when you listen to your soul. Whatever approach you take, it must help you get in touch with your soul. It's whispering to you all the time, and you have to listen to what is being said.

But *why* do you need to listen to your Whispering Soul?

Because it is the most important voice in your life. It needs to be nourished.

Taking the quiet time is necessary so that the only sound we are listening to is the core self, the Whispering Soul. For happiness and soul contentment, we need to give ourselves time to find out who we are and to do that we need to hear what our soul is telling us.

If we don't listen to what it is saying, the deepest spiritual areas of our life will be neglected. If this happens, then in my opinion, we can become ill. This may be a physical, emotional, mental or spiritual illness, but this continued failure to listen to the soul, the authentic self needs, to be avoided. We won't be able to heal easily if we repeatedly ignore our soul. It will make it harder, certainly. I believe any escape route we are taking is because there's something inside that's actually crying out to heal. But there's nothing outside of us that's going to heal the problem, only ourselves.

I am very aware in the quiet time that my soul is whispering to me. I can hear the whisper and I can resonate with what it is telling me; having said that, if I am not listening properly, my soul is going to shout at me, especially if there is something it needs me to hear. I prefer to hear it from a whisper than from a shout.

We need to find our authentic self and find solutions. I have certainly had to in my life as you now know. No matter how spiritual we become on this planet, life is going to throw us lessons. When we have relationships of any kind, we will be presented with challenges and lessons. We are all in relationships: we go to the shop and buy groceries – that is a relationship with the person we are giving money to, there's a connection going on there. Just now I took a break from writing and went for a nice walk, and along the way I bumped into a walker and a little black and white dog that I petted. That's another relationship there. No matter where we go in our journey, we are having relationships.

That quiet time calms your mind and then answers and ideas will come forward. Maybe you have issues in a relationship? Listen to your soul in this way and the confusion will fade away and you will see a solution. Maybe you need to change the way you are communicating? I find you might not even be consciously aware of the soul advising you at first, but it will be there, whispering, helping.

For example, so many people come to me and they say that the problem they are experiencing is to do with a relationship, or maybe even several relationships. This is totally common. Usually it is a breakdown of some kind in that relationship that is causing problems. A typical scenario might be a busy young family where the husband and wife both work and have children. They are both so busy getting ready for work, getting the kids ready, getting all the endless jobs done every day that they rarely if ever find time to communicate. Maybe they get successful and then get a big house, a nice car, expensive holidays and nice clothes. There might even be a nanny. But the husband is working long hours to pay for all these things and they are both so exhausted by the end of each day that they never really talk to each other. Often the husband is working so hard he doesn't have time to be with the children, never mind his wife. They both need to step back from this and listen to their souls.

Part of the problem here is that we often expect too much of relationships. What I mean by this is that we *expect* the other person to make us happy. When they don't, it causes problems. But what I have discovered over the many years I have had to work on myself is that nobody can make me happy, only *me*. I know this is easier to write and say than to do, but it's a simple fact. If you are waiting for someone else to make you happy and everything perfect, you may be waiting a very long time. In terms of relationships, if you are not even having communication with yourself, how can you expect to have any with other people? If you give your soul a chance to tell you what you need, then communicating with others will be so much easier. And, more fruitful.

Please don't get me wrong, I can bring out and share my happiness and of course it's very enjoyable to share someone else's contentment, but if I am waiting for someone else to make me happy I am going to be in trouble.

And how do you make yourself happy? By listening to others?

No.

Listen to your Whispering Soul. The answers lie within.

You only need ten, maybe fifteen minutes a day. And the rewards will be incredible. However if you could manage thirty minutes, the results could be so much better.

CHAPTER 11

AN OLD LADY IN
A MARKET

When we had the bakery in Kimmage and lived above it, we used to go to the early morning covered market to get supplies for the week. We'd stock up on the baking ingredients we needed, but we also used to buy a few flowers, some soups and lots of other things that we liked to sell in the shop. Each week we went to get all these goodies and Dermot would go and pick a trolley while I started looking for items off the list.

On one particular day, I had the cash and I sent Dermot off to get our trolley. As I turned to start walking around the market, I noticed an old lady picking food up off the floor. She was scouring the ground, picking up scraps of food and then cleaning it off with her own dirty fingers, pulling bits of grit or rubbish off the food before hurriedly eating it.

I walked over and she seemed a little surprised that anyone had even noticed her.

'Are you okay there?' I asked gently.

'I'm grand, thanks.'

She wasn't grand. She was very unkempt, smelly and looked absolutely worn out.

'Where are you living right now?'

'Oh, sometimes I get into the overnight hostel and sometimes I sleep here in the market.'

I asked her what had happened that had left her sleeping in a covered food market. She explained to me that she had once been married but after her husband died, things had started to go wrong. Her daughter had gone to live in Australia and got married to someone there, while she had got herself into money troubles and eventually been evicted. She didn't want her daughter to know and cause upset, or make her move back, away from her new life in Australia, so she'd kept quiet and got on with the life of a homeless person on her own. Within a year or so, she'd lost all contact with her daughter and had no money and no ability to get back in touch.

She was telling me this and I was looking at her, listening intently. She was probably in her sixties but looked much, much older.

'Can I get you a cup of tea and we can carry on our chat?' I offered.

'Oh, no thank you, I don't really want them to notice me. I like to be invisible.'

I stood there next to this woman, thinking about my own troubles back at the bakery, my own childhood and all the millions of thoughts swirling around my head. Then I made a decision.

I took the entire week's cash out of my pocket. It was the equivalent of about 250 Euros.

'Look, my name is Betty Cosgrave. I'm giving you this money, now. Here's my phone number too and if you ever need anything else, you call this and I will help.'

Something was telling me I had to give this woman all our money. Bear in mind we were pretty much living hand to mouth ourselves, albeit with a roof over our heads. The cash I had pulled from my pocket was all we had spare for the week's stock. Without stock we couldn't sell anything or make any money. I knew all of this but I just had to give her the money. I was compelled to do it.

She took the money, looked at the crumpled notes in her wrinkled and dirty hands and then looked up at me.

'Why are you doing this? Why have you given me this money?'

'I just know it's going to help you.'

While all this was going on, Dermot had collected a trolley and was busy filling it with all the stock we needed for the week ahead.

But now we had no money to buy it with.

The old lady went on her way and I caught up with Dermot. He'd seen me talking to the old lady and casually asked, 'Betty, have you been giving the old lady a few bob?'

'I gave her the whole lot.'

'What do you mean "the whole lot?"'

'I gave her all of our money; I had to.'

'How are we going to manage? We need to buy stock. I can't believe you did that!'

'I know, you're right. But I had to give it to her. *My soul was crying out to me to give her the money.* We'll get the money from somewhere, we'll find a way.'

Dermot was used to me by then. He was used to me giving money away, although usually if I had say IR£50, I'd give someone IR£30.

About a year later, the phone rang and a woman's voice asked to speak to Betty Cosgrave.

'That's me, who's speaking please?'

It was the old lady from the covered market.

I was really taken aback but as soon as I regained my composure I asked after her and enquired what she'd been up to.

She explained to me that she had taken my money that day in the market, got herself washed and cleaned up with some nice new clothes and started sleeping at the hostel in a safer environment. Within a few days, she'd got some help tracking down where her daughter had moved to on the other side of the world and immediately got back in touch.

Her daughter was overwhelmed to hear from her mother.

The little old lady in the market was calling me from Australia, where she lived in a lovely family home, reunited with her daughter.

PART III

TIPS &
TECHNIQUES

Now you know how that little girl from a council estate grew to be able to write the book which you hold in your hands, it's time for me to offer you a few insights and ideas of tips and techniques that may help you as much as they have helped me and my clients.

Some of the tips in this section are little life lessons, common sense ideas that I like to pass on that can have a huge positive impact, even though they may seem quite simple. Other techniques are established ideas from a number of schools of thought, such as Neuro-Linguistic Programming (NLP), Reiki and Kinesiology. These are techniques that I have come across, researched and learned more about and offer up to you as an introductory insight into various ways of improving your life and thinking. At the end of the book, there are details of where to find out more information about these schools of thought, should you wish to. I live these techniques, just like taking a breath and I have used all of them on my clients at one time or another.

For readers who feel they haven't the strength to make these changes, I say it's not about your character. It's about the tools. They helped me get strength. And most importantly of all, it's the *repetition* of using the tools that will bolster you and help you make progress. I have discovered with myself that my day-to-day life is fine yet I can go somewhere and a smell might trigger an emotion, and *instantly* I am caught. However because I have immersed myself into the repetition of taking quiet time and using some of these tools, I can take a couple of seconds and quickly know what the emotion is and deal with that.

I still use the tools, I still live with depression but what I do now is I manage it. I separate that out as one unit of my life but I don't take it into every area of my life and feel bad about everything. I say, *This is one area that needs to be looked at but all these other areas are great.* So be objective about your life, don't worry about everything you do, there may only be one certain aspect that needs working on.

The over-riding and single most important suggestion I can make, however, is this: *you need to learn to manage your thoughts.* Throughout my childhood and certainly very much as an adult making my way through the various experiences you've read about, managing my thoughts has been the single biggest challenge to me, over and over again.

I am very careful with my thoughts. There are thousands of books about the effects of positive thinking. Likewise, negative thinking is just as powerful. The brain is very much like a computer and, in simple terms, if you programme it with negative ideas, those thoughts become your reality. At the precise moment you are having a thought, to your brain that is a reality. If your belief system keeps telling you that you are no good, then eventually – if that thought remains unchallenged – the belief will become reality.

This journey is about our own inner self and no matter what challenges you have outside with relationships, or work, or children or money, whatever it is, the biggest challenge every individual has is their own thoughts. This affects directly how we react to challenges, how we process them and therefore how we respond to them.

All these tools can help: many of them are common sense; others are based on complex theories. The point is they will help you break out of patterns of behaviour and help you manage your thoughts. Now, it may take time, but the crucial thing is to make sure it *stops*. Stick with it and above all, live it. It is your brain, no one else's. Make that happen.

Here's some great ideas to get you started.

IN THE SHOWER

At the time of writing, people are facing grave financial problems all over the world. Each day millions of people will be waking up anxious, worried about the day ahead and what it might bring. Many of my clients are very successful, highly paid executives who come to me in a very stressed state. These people – like many others – will wake up in the morning with a terrible sense of gloom and doom already in their heads, as soon as they open their eyes.

If this sounds like you, here is a very simple tip.

Take a hot shower.

I realise this isn't exactly rocket science, but there is a very good reason for this.

Let me explain. You get in the shower and literally start washing yourself but you can add to that physical process by thinking of the water hitting your back, splashing off your head and your shoulders and washing off all the negativity. At first we are clogged by the thoughts in our brain and the worry and anxiety that is muddying our mind. So stand under the shower for a few moments and calm your breathing. Consciously feel the water cleansing these worries away, then add a little visualisation in there too, feel the troubles wash down your spine and front, down your legs and into the shower tray, then down into the plughole and away. Then immediately replace these negatives with positives, the things you need to do today to make a difference, to move forward, things you know you can do and that will make a difference. If you cleanse the body externally in this way, you will also be cleansing the mind from within.

Stay in for at least ten or fifteen minutes, thinking, visualising, relaxing. This has the added benefit of shutting you off from the world for a little while, it gives you chance to hear your soul, away from the TV, the mobile phone, the office ...

Maybe you already do this without even realising it?

Have you ever had a shower and said afterwards, 'Oh, I feel better for that!'?

Try it.

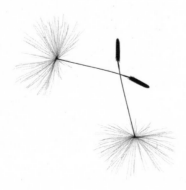

THE EARLY BIRD

If you have a difficult call to make or maybe a tricky meeting to attend, if at all possible schedule it for first thing in the morning. There is no point waiting until the end of the day when you've had another eight hours of work to tire you out. By then you will have been worrying about the meeting all day and may have lost a clear focus or perspective. Steel yourself for the meeting or call, make it early and you will feel a clear benefit.

If there's a situation within your family or a key relationship that is the cause of your worry, you can do the same. Meet for early morning coffee maybe. If you look after a family, then it's maybe not possible to rush out of the house at 9am to speak to someone, but as soon as you are able, sit down and have that chat. Why put yourself in a corner where you have to manage your thoughts for six hours when you can simply change your schedule and only have to manage them for one hour? A day is a long time to be anxious about a meeting; if you cut down on the time spent waiting and worrying, you cut down on the anxiety; if you cut down on the anxiety, it is healthier and you will be calmer and more focused; if you are calmer and more focused, it is far more likely that there will be a resolution when you meet up. And then you will have the rest of the day to enjoy yourself!

FOOD AND DRINK

Here's a common sense tip that so many people ignore. Drink water. The pace of life is so fast, people rush around in meetings, school runs, shopping, visiting relatives, it's all so hectic. That's fine, that's life, but there are a few very simple things you can do to help yourself along the way. It is a clinical fact that if you are dehydrated you will feel less capable, your concentration will drop and, crucially, your mood may well be affected in a negative way.

You should drink six to eight glasses of water a day. It's vital.

This needs to be clear water, don't include tea or coffee, or even herbal teas in that count. Just water. This water will get your oxygenated blood flowing and keep your body hydrated. This will give your brain more energy. This in turn will make you far more likely to manage your thoughts.

So many people don't take the time to do it and there's really no excuse. Nowadays you can buy a bottle of water from almost anywhere, so even if you are rushing around, you can drink plenty. One nice tip is to try a cup of warm water in the morning; I feel that really helps get you going at the start of the day. And don't mistake thirst for hunger. Often, you might think you are hungry but a nice cool glass of water is actually all you need. This is particularly important if food is an issue for you in some way.

It's not just drinking enough water that people can neglect. With food, there are obviously more serious problems with over- or under-eating (those are related to emotional issues), but a more everyday mistake that can be easily solved is eating too fast. We've all done it, rushing to a meeting or a train or bus and we need a bite to eat, so we grab something (usually fairly slimy!) from a shop and eat it as we rush around, literally chewing on the go. Even if you are not actually walking when you eat, most of us have wolfed down a sandwich on the move for some reason. Some people do this as part of their daily routine, they maybe pass a sandwich shop on the way to work and eat it as they walk. Worse still, they are probably buying food that is far from ideal in terms of what nutrition it is providing.

Stop eating on the go!

If at all possible, when you buy a sandwich, try to find somewhere to sit down and eat it. It might be a park bench or it might be in your car, that's fine, but *take your time*. Be conscious of your breathing as you eat, practice eating and breathing very slowly, it might feel a little forced and weird at first but after a while it will become second nature. In my view, this simple remedy will give your brain the chance to connect with what you are doing, with what you are literally putting in your mouth. That's why sometimes you might rush a sandwich down but feel hungry ten minutes later – your brain hasn't had chance to register what you did. Some clients of mine have even reported eating the same food but losing weight, because they aren't snacking in between meals due to this hunger. Of course, the other bonus is that if you eat properly you will have more focus and brain power.

Some people say to me that their boss pressures them into eating on the go and rushing their lunch. An awful lot of people don't even take lunch at all anymore or they are eating at their desk. I recognise that every job has its pressures and office politics are tricky sometimes, but the simple fact is you are legally required to have a lunch break. When clients of mine actually start taking responsibility for their own physical, mental and spiritual health and take only fifteen minutes away from the desk or, better still, walk round the block at lunch, then they get twice as much work done that afternoon. There is a shift into a healthier mental state. Within three days, your boss will see how much more productive and focused you are, so then he or she won't mind.

I find that if people have instant hunger and they feel like they have to eat right *now*, that's emotional hunger; conversely, if they are actually physically hungry, the body is going to actually let them know subtly at first. There'll be a little groaning in the gut that will get louder and then they get weak. That's physical hunger but if it's instant there's an emotion going on that they may need to step back from.

The logic of listening to your soul absolutely can apply to issues that you may think are physical – like food addiction for instance. If someone is escaping through food - if they are not just eating the chocolate because they enjoy the chocolate, then they are suppressing something, it means there is some emotional or mental issue going on inside of them. If they don't take the time out – whether that's with a therapist or with themselves – to find out what that emotion is, they are not going to be able to resolve that issue. Food is one of the most difficult compulsions to stop, simply because we all have to eat. We are therefore faced with the ritual of eating more than once a day.

Food affects our mood so directly, so powerfully – especially poor quality food, processed food and junk. You feel bad so you grab a burger on the run then within twenty minutes you are having a fast food crash and the cycle repeats itself. You don't need to be a nutritionist to see that is an unhelpful and potentially damaging cycle, both mentally and physically. How will you manage your thoughts if you can barely keep your eyes open?

If food is not actually an issue for you, that doesn't mean that you should treat it lightly. You need to prioritise eating decent, healthy food, *slowly*. It's common sense, but do you always do this?

Well, start right now.

TAPPING

Here's the first of my tips taken from one of the areas of expertise I have trained myself in over the years. Tapping is an idea originally mooted by Dr Roger Callaghan, a Californian psychologist in the 1980s. Dr Wayne Topping has also been at the forefront of this area of work – his pioneering ideas showed executives how to use techniques such as this to cope with and overcome stress (I have actually trained with Wayne Topping himself). However, Tapping is one of those techniques that I came to as an adult but later realised that I had been unconsciously doing similar techniques since I was a very young child.

If I take you back to the house in Ledwidge Crescent, whenever I had a bad experience or a shock, as you know I would sit there rocking back and forth. But I would also tap my hands, repetitively over and over, it gave me reassurance. Obviously I didn't know anything at all about pressure points or so-called 'Meridian systems', but I would sit there rocking back and forth and I would tap in a rhythm with one hand on the back of the other. I would almost go into a state of hypnosis, a state of calm, then all of a sudden – usually within a few minutes – whatever I was scared about was gone. That is essentially what Tapping is about and all those years ago I was doing that naturally as a child.

A specific example for me that comes to mind immediately is to do with my father. As you know, he was home visiting once a year and when he came to the house, I'd listen out for his movements, to see if he was going out or staying in. When I realised he was staying in, I would feel pure panic from my toes to the top of my head and my body would start vibrating and I would rock. If he started his pipe or rolling his cigarettes, I knew that meant he wasn't going out and that smell remains one of my most powerful and upsetting triggers to this day. I had nowhere to go because I was too small, I might have got away briefly but he'd look for me. So the panic would hit me and I would rock and tap, rock and tap and within seconds I wouldn't even notice the smell, I'd feel so calm and so relaxed.

As a child I was consciously aware of my rocking and tapping, I knew it was something I did even though people might see it and think it was involuntary; however, although I knew it was soothing, it wasn't until much later in life when I read about the ideas of people like Dr Callaghan and Dr Wayne Topping that I realised there was more to it.

Now it is a technique I use a lot with my clients.

The basic premise of Tapping is that the body has various pressure points which are directly related to your well-being and your actual organs. This may be a physical, mental or emotional issue but certain Tapping techniques can help resolve those problems. To help you learn more about Tapping, I've put some references at the back of this book, but for the purpose of this section, let me give you one example of a technique that you may be able to use on yourself very quickly and with potentially great results.

The pressure points I've mentioned are indeed related to organs or systems in the body where we hold a lot of emotions. For example, the stomach is considered by many to be related to anxiety and stress. Now, in Tapping, the Meridian that is connected to the stomach is found in the area below the eyes. There's a cycle that goes through that Meridian system and it has an electrical current with a 35-second cycle. So how do you use this to alleviate stress?

Well, you stay in touch with the particular negative emotion that is troubling you and evaluate it on a scale of nought to ten. If it's really heightened and stressful, maybe a panic attack, then it's an eight, or nine. If it's something that troubles you periodically and only moderately, then maybe it's a five. You simply stay in touch with that emotion and tap under both eyes at the same time, with the middle and index fingers 35 times. By the time you get to 35, that emotion will have probably scaled back down to a six or five. Go back and tap it again for another 35 seconds, it'll be down to a four or three. Then go back in again for 35 seconds more and it will be gone. If this is done properly, it is like pressing the Delete button on the computer, it's that good.

Other Tapping techniques might use the pinky finger or other acupressure points, I have just given you one very simple technique, but there are many, many more. It's a fascinating area and one I have used personally and professionally with great reward. It worked for me as a child; it works for me as an adult; it will work for you, if *you* work it.

BREATHING

Possibly the most important tip I will ever give you is about breathing. This is something I've already touched on when I spoke about your Whispering Soul. It sounds odd because breathing is obviously something that is crucial to our existence, but the sad fact is that many, many people are only breathing in a shallow and short way. I've noticed a lot of clients who tell me they get very angry in traffic and easily wound up are actually breathing too shallow. They are getting this anxious and angry at many times during each day, but it is most noticeable when they are driving. They are simply not getting enough oxygenated blood into their body. This can make you anxious. It's a fact.

What you need to do is learn to be consciously aware of your breathing.

Sit down now without any distractions around you and breathe in.

Take a deep breath in through your nose, count to four – and as you do, be aware of the cold air going through the nostrils and into your lungs and stomach – hold for the count of four and then breathe out through the nostrils, again being consciously aware of the warm air going out of the nose. Feel the air being sucked into your nostrils, going through and into your body, visualise it surging into your lungs and stomach and filling them with oxygen, then feel the oxygen rushing around your body and giving it all that precious energy. Make sure the breath is going right in, filling the lungs, right into your diaphragm; then when you exhale, make sure it is from the stomach.

This simple ritual will relax you immediately.

GRATITUDE

This is one of the single most important tips in my book.

Gratitude.

So many of us have so much to be thankful for, yet we overlook this and concentrate on the negatives. But if you are in gratitude, you can't be feeling sorry for yourself. A positive outweighs a negative.

Now, you can't be in gratitude all the time, it's not a human state. But you can form a habit where you instinctively revert to gratitude and reflect on why you can feel grateful for what you have.

There is nobody on this planet who has not been challenged at some point or another.

A young man who is taking drugs.

A young mother who struggles to show her beloved child physical affection.

Someone who is bereaved.

Someone who is struggling financially.

Someone who is ill or has someone they love who is ill.

There are all sorts of challenges and lots of people find themselves in many difficult situations. What we can do is to somehow never lose sight of the things we have that we can be grateful for. They are blessings, gifts, and we need to keep those close to our heart. They will nourish our soul.

One way of doing this is to keep a Gratitude Journal.

Some of my clients might leave a session with me in a really contented and healthy state of mind but they can't control the people and places around them as soon as they walk out through my door into the wider world. They might immediately come across someone or something that makes them unhappy or troubled. That is always going to happen, you have to acknowledge that. There's a lot of negativity around. This can make it hard to hold on to and cherish the happy thoughts. I am a *very* contented person and have huge and regular bursts of happiness. However, I know many people who live with depression who don't enjoy those bursts of contentment, and that is really sad.

However, we can remind ourselves of the great blessings in our life with a simple Gratitude Journal. Go and buy yourself a nice little note book, it doesn't need to be expensive (mine are often from the Pound Shop). Then start keeping a daily Gratitude Journal. At the end of each day, write down what has happened that you are grateful for.

I'll give you a personal example. On a trip to England recently on business, my last meeting went very well and I was able to head towards my grandson's home for a visit quite a lot earlier than I had arranged. In fact I was able to phone ahead to Fran and arrange to pick up Josh from school.

My grandson wasn't expecting us to pick him up from school and so seeing Josh's face when we were there, waiting for him at the school gates was absolutely wonderful! We took a lovely little photograph of him with us there and then, and I have put that in my Gratitude Journal next to the written entry for that special moment. It was such a simple thing but such a lovely loving reaction. He was ecstatic! Remembering that and looking at the photograph makes me feel extremely grateful. Nothing could give me more pleasure.

Human beings have a tendency to think about what they haven't achieved, rather than what they have. Well, on that day, getting to Josh's school early and seeing his beautiful little face light up when he saw me and Dermot was a fantastic experience and so that's why I made a note of it in my own Gratitude Journal.

The day after, we spent the whole time with Josh, we went shopping and walking by the river and all day he was making little comments and making us laugh, he was saying the sweetest little things. In the afternoon we were just kicking a ball in the park – that's all, just simply kicking a ball around – and Josh came up to me and said, 'Nan, this is great!' I could have exploded with happiness! I was so grateful for that little affirmation. Straight in the Journal with that one, Josh!

The same can apply to your profession too. That very same week, I took a phone call from a client who'd previously been made redundant and I'd been coaching her on getting a great new job. She'd had two big interviews coming up and we'd been researching the companies, I'd been talking her through the interview situation, preparing for the questions and the pressures that come with all that. Then she phoned me and said she'd been offered a job by both companies. I was so grateful that I had been part of someone's solution like that. Into my Journal it went (you'll hear more from this lady, Nessa, later in the book).

By the way, I always buy quite small note books for my Journal, because then you can pop this in your bag or jacket and carry it with you always; then if you want to make a new entry, it's right to hand and there's no chance of you forgetting or neglecting to write down something which was wonderful. Like me, some clients have put photographs in there too. It's up to you, it's your Journal.

A few weeks after Nessa phoned me, I was out walking when I saw a fox. Now a lot of foxes you see are underfed, skinny and not very colourful, but this particular one was bright and bushy, he was a startling red and obviously very healthy and full of life. He stood there and I'm sure he looked at me, I even thought I caught a smile! Seriously though, he didn't run away, there was no fear, he just sort of acknowledged I was there and then trotted off. Again, straight in the Journal.

Those are just a few recent examples of entries from my own Gratitude Journal. What you put in your Journal is entirely up to you. Even the smallest, seemingly trivial thing can be mentioned, as long as it makes you feel grateful for the wonderful things in your life. Your Gratitude Journal will become a part of your ritual, it will become second nature to pull it out and jot something lovely down, and over time that little note book will grow and grow and feed your positive outlook on life.

A NEGATIVE THOUGHT FAST

A technique I learned from Paul McKenna – that is used by several schools of thought such as 'Thought Field Therapy' – is a so-called Negative Thought Fast. Negative thoughts create negative feelings in our body and can create pain and ultimately illness. They can also severely affect how we communicate which in turn dismantles our relationships and also our ability to manage our mind. Negative thoughts have to be dealt with. Never underestimate the damage they can cause if you don't manage them.

How I would personally use this approach on clients is by asking them to fast for a week from negative thoughts. Your Gratitude Journal will be a key part of this. You can take it a step further in the week of your negative thought fast – one night, write on a slip of paper what you are grateful for that day, then stick this under your pillow when you go to bed. As soon as you wake up the next day, take the slip of paper out and read it, dwell on the positive thoughts and gratitude that this note creates. Start the day with gratitude. Then take a moment to ask yourself how you *feel* with gratitude and how you felt when you were having those positive thoughts.

That morning, write down at least four positive thoughts. If any negative thoughts crop up in your mind, dismiss them and immediately replace them with a positive from your list. Say to yourself, *I am on a fast from negative thoughts*. Do the same each day and by the end of the week, between your Journal and your pillow notes, you will have plenty of positive thoughts to replace any negative ones!

Again, keep notes or your Journal in your pocket so they are there ready to be used if a negative thought creeps up on you. We are only human and so, for example, if you work in an office, the period of eight hours in a working day is definitely going to provoke negative thoughts. Do not allow them in – *I am on a fast from negative thoughts.*

As an aside from the Negative Thought Fast, with more complex issues I have sometimes asked clients to sign a contract. The problem needs more than just a personal intent to avoid negative thoughts. So I write up a simple one page agreement that states very clearly what they will and will not do, what they acknowledge is an unwelcome pattern of behaviour and states that they agree – by signing the contract – to stop that. However, a contract is rather more severe – a personal Negative Thought Fast is often sufficient to stop the majority of people's repetitive patterns.

Work at it; initially the negative thoughts will battle hard to clutter your mind and prevent you from feeling positive. Persevere. You might have two or three attempts at lasting a week but you will get there. You need to manage your thoughts.

I promise if you do this and do the Negative Thought Fast for an entire week, the results will be profound. That week will start off a whole new lifestyle of positive thinking.

BURNING PAPER

When I was growing up, I never thought I had any right to have any feelings – whether that was sadness, anger, jealousy, happiness, or whatever. Nobody sat me down and explained what to do if I felt angry or sad. So dealing with emotions was something of a mystery to me. As I grew older, this particularly showed up when I was angry. When I came in touch with anger I personally had to learn a new way of dealing with it. As I trained in various disciplines, I realised that I needed to work through this and find a way to manage it better.

As a general observation, it is important that anger is acknowledged, the mental acknowledgement helps you draw the anger out of your body and the mind without hurting ourselves or anyone else. That is all very well, but that's easier to say than to sometimes do.

So here's a tip to help that process.

Write down all your angry thoughts on a piece of paper. You might be angry about all sorts of things, people, money, your career. Whatever it is, write it down and really let rip! Say the things you really would like to say, even the thoughts you know are over the top and really incredibly angry. Write them all down.

No one is going to read this note except you so don't hold back.

Then put the note in an envelope, address it to the full postal address of the person with whom you are angry.

Then put a first class stamp on it.

Then burn it.

This might sound odd but what it does is help you gather up all that anger – which is really serving you no purpose at all – and takes it out of your head.

You can do this with other emotions too; I've found it works best with anger, but if you find the letter can describe your sadness or resentment or jealousy and that burning it dissipates this, then that's your solution.

DISASSOCIATION AND VISUALISATION

Here are techniques that will help you manage your thoughts and keep negative emotions from embedding themselves in your mind. I learned these during my many courses and they are used in various ways by many disciplines (including NLP, which was originated by Dr Richard Bandler and John Grinder) and used widely for releasing negative thoughts, letting go of a situation and replacing it with a positive one. This is based on the principle that you get more of what you associate into and, conversely, less of what you disassociate from. However, like Tapping, I realised that it was something I had been doing a variation of, in my own childlike way, when I was distressed as a little girl. Again, I didn't have a word for these habits I formed but these schools of thought have given me labels and shown me many other ways of using these ideas.

If you think a thought, it becomes a reality. What you associate into, you get more of. Therefore, it follows that what you disassociate from, you will get less of. As a little girl, I use to have the thought, *I'm not good enough, I'm not good enough*, circling round in my head, over and over and over.

One of the things that comes to mind for me now would be my mum. When I was a bit cheeky and annoying her, asking after when she was coming back from work or the slots or wherever (I only wanted my mum back, that's all), she had a habit of eventually saying, 'If you keep on, I am never going to come home. I will never come back. I will never come home.' And she'd repeat that over and over.

Then she'd go out and that sentence would be burned into my brain so that I would say it over and over in my head too. If I was really introverted one day, I'd sit for hours in a dark room, not wanting to go out, just repeating that sentence over again.

Then I started to disassociate. I wouldn't have called it that but I'd sit alone rocking, the thought would come in, 'She's never going to come home, she's never going to come back,' and then I'd go back into a pleasant thought. I would see this upsetting thought going away from me and disappearing. Here is a step-by-step explanation to help you get a clear understanding of this technique:

1. Think of a positive situation, one in which you felt positive about yourself. Such as when you got your exams, passed your driving test, etc.

2. Sitting comfortably, close your eyes, feet flat on the floor, hands on your lap.

3. In your mind's eye, picture a blank canvas out in front of you. Place the situation you want to disassociate from into this canvas, including any negative emotions that may go with it (you can picture a rainbow coming up from your belly-button through your solar plexus and out into the picture if this helps to release the emotions).

4. Spend a few moments doing this.

5. When it's all out in the canvas, drain the colour from the picture.

6. Now picture it becoming smaller and smaller, moving away from your body into the distance, until it's disappeared into the horizon.

7. Put another blank canvas in front of you, this time it's the

positive situation you want to associate into.

8. Put all the colours, vibrations, even music into it, things that you love.

9. Make it the size of a football pitch.

10. Bring it in towards you.

11. Now either step into it or have it associate into you.

12. Engulf yourself in the amazing positive emotions, see what you saw, hear what you heard, feel what you felt.

13. Slowly open your eyes.

14. Repeat if necessary.

I was very good at visualizing as a child, it was just something that came naturally to me. I was left to my own devices so much, I suppose. One ritual I used was seeing the nasty thought coming out of my eyes and floating away then disappearing. I often replaced the nasty sentence or thought with nice thoughts, like the arthritic lady Kate, or Patricia or someone who might have showed me some kindness. I'd see Kate walking towards me and then I'd feel the nice emotions going through me. Then I'd usually go to sleep and be nice and comfy and when I woke up the next morning, my mother would be home.

Visualisation is used widely by numerous disciplines such as NLP and is a great way to manage your thoughts. It's okay to remove a negative thought from your mind, but if you don't replace it with anything, there is a void, a vacuum and that will almost definitely be replaced by new negative thoughts unless you fill it with something positive. Visualisation is worthy of a book on its own, but for the purpose here, let me give you an example of a client I worked with who was very ill indeed. She's called Chloe and she is a beautiful young girl who you will meet again later in the book.

She'd suffered severe abuse and I worked with her after stints in two mental hospitals. The specific example of visualisation I'd like to show you is this. Chloe had disconnected with her soul, she had lost touch with her core self and was self-harming badly. So, in one of the first sessions we did, I used visualisation where I asked Chloe to imagine that she was walking up a beautiful mountain and along the way I asked her to notice that there was a lovely stream, gently flowing along on her left-hand side. In the stream was a leaf and it seemed to be expanding as she got closer to it. I had her stop and watch the leaf as it grew and then I suggested that she imagine a rainbow, travelling from her heart over to the leaf and told her that she could use this rainbow to transport any pain or suffering that she felt, over to the leaf. Next I asked her to turn and watch, as the leaf floated down the stream, carrying with it all of her pain. I asked her to continue her journey up the mountain but said that now she would feel lighter because of what she had unburdened. I told her that once she reached the summit, she was going to meet her soul self, who was waiting there to be reconnected with her. This was the beautiful, childlike and innocent Chloe, who was full of dreams and ambitions and was longing to be reconnected. Once she reached the top, she found a seat and sat down. I told her to look over to her right and she would see her soul self waiting for her and if she listened carefully, she would hear her soul self whisper to her of all the wonderful journeys they would make together. I told her that she could choose at that moment to find new ways to express her pain from now on and she had no need to use cutting any longer. I left her in quiet contemplation of this for a while and suggested she make her way back down the mountain.

The techniques I have learned from schools such as NLP are extensive and here is not the place to detail them fully, but you can read more from the contacts at the back of this book.

FINDING TIME FOR YOURSELF

For most of my life I have looked to make other people happy. I can see where this came from. I had chronic abandonment issues as a child and that often manifests itself in a desire to please others. When those kids ran down the hill to greet my mum and get sweets off her after she'd won on the slots, I didn't think, *Why is Mum doing that?* I thought, *There must be something really wrong with me. What can I change to please her?*

For years, I almost became obsessive-compulsive in trying to make other people happy. I didn't know how to live on the planet unless I was out doing something for somebody else. I didn't know how to just 'be'. That is not only exhausting, but ultimately if that is done at the expense of any regard for ourselves, we will burn out and be less rewarding to know for all those people that you've spent so much time trying to please.

So the last few years, that's what I've been doing, I've been looking at what makes me happy too. I have to find happiness within myself before I start sharing it with others. I need to be able to take care of my own needs before I can look after anyone else's.

So take a little time to sit back and think about what you need yourself. Maybe you don't get enough time to read a book? Or you want to keep a little fitter? Perhaps you want to spend more time playing with the children rather than doing chores? Or perhaps your parents place unreasonable demands on you and you neglect both yourself and your partner by trying to meet those requests. There are, of course, a million and one questions like this, but unless you find some time to hear yourself – again this is your soul whispering to you – you will never know.

If you have children, this will probably go against your instinct; I am not suggesting for one second you put yourself before them, but if you don't give time to yourself, you will not be as happy and contented in your own life and that will reflect in theirs too. Taking time for yourself will benefit everyone around you. If you do, you will become a much better person, a better parent, a better partner, friend and work colleague.

TIME OUT

Whatever circumstances you are in, you will be experiencing all sorts of emotions: happiness, sadness, anger, frustration, self-pity, a whole world of feelings. The problem with many of these emotions is that they are negative and if you let them play over and over in your mind for longer than you should, they will become very destructive. This next tip might sound easier to suggest than to actually do, and in some ways that is certainly true, but again with practice you will get better and better and find that it really is possible to manage your thoughts this precisely.

Let's use a very common emotion – self-pity. You wake up one day and for whatever reason, maybe a very legitimate one or maybe just a general melancholy, you feel sorry for yourself. What I suggest is that you acknowledge the emotion, you say you are feeling sorry for yourself, then put a time limit on it. Look at your watch and think, *Okay, I am giving myself fifteen minutes to feel this emotion. I'll feel sorry for myself and wallow in that, allow those feelings to express themselves and be dominant in my mind; if there's still a need after that then I will give myself another five minutes, but then that is that.*

If it's a real biggie, give yourself half an hour, but no more.

By acknowledging the emotion, you are not suppressing it, you are not ignoring it. You are not denying your feelings, you are airing them and letting them breathe. You are allowing them to be felt and thought about; however – and this is crucial – you are not allowing that negative emotion to drag on and on, because if you do that you will get caught up in it for too long.

Reading this may sound very simplistic, overly simplistic even, but trust me, if you keep at this, it can really work. Just as a negative thought can repeat and repeat and repeat, burying itself deep in your mind with that cycle, then likewise a habit like this can cut that cycle short and make it hugely less damaging.

A neat trick is to actually get a little travel clock that you use just for this purpose. You'll have it in a drawer and when you feel you need to put a cap on a negative feeling or emotion, take the clock out and set the alarm to fifteen minutes.

And at the end of the fifteen minutes when that alarm beeps?

Come back to gratitude.

BREAK THE CIRCLE

Like the section on gratitude, this is one of the most important points I have to make in this book.

Many negative patterns of behaviour are actually just a repetition of something seen or learned in childhood or adulthood. I've lost count of the times I've heard someone who has been behaving in an inappropriate way using a previous experience as some kind of catch-all excuse. Of course, in some instances, there is a very good reason why that person was unable to break away and stop the circle repeating. I am not making light of the more severe problems people suffer; however, in many cases, so many of us choose to repeat patterns of behaviour that could actually be stopped. They could be ended, there and then.

I know this from personal experience. Remember when I couldn't cuddle my beautiful little son, Fran? That was a pattern of behaviour I had learned. I had been around that coldness and I couldn't initially react differently.

But I did. I changed.

I broke the circle.

Admittedly I had to work at it because it was so alien to me at first, as you've seen. But I looked at what practical steps I could take to help me overcome the emotional hurdle – hence the crèche visits and parenting classes. I'd actually say that this was the biggest pattern I've broken in my life. As I mentioned, I could have said, 'This is because of my parents and I know it isn't right, however it's just the way I am ...' but I didn't. I thought to myself, *Not only is my child going to suffer here, but I am going to miss out on this beautiful connection too.*

This is just a specific and personal example but there is a wider point to be made here about breaking the circle. Think about this: if you don't break the circle, the negative pattern of behaviour will be replicated on and on and on, and your own ability to stop this cyclical process has gone. However, if you are the one person in your family who decides – maybe after several generations – that enough is enough and the circle has to be broken, then you have just made a colossal impact on future generations of your family. The specific details of the circle you want to break are private to you and you may need some or all of the tools and tips I have explained here – plus others perhaps – but it is a goal that is incredibly worthwhile and important.

Because it stops there and then, the pattern of behaviour is no more. And then that great leap forward is down to you. What greater achievement can there be?

Now my little Fran, the happy gorgeous three-year-old bouncing up for a cuddle with his mummy is a great big man with a child of his own and another one on the way – and guess what? You'll never meet a more tactile, cuddly daddy in your life, he hugs his little boy Josh, throws him up in the air, tickles him, chases him and growls at him until he roars with laughter, it's the most natural and most enjoyable thing in the world to him and he never even thinks about it.

The circle has been broken.

TAKE RESPONSIBILITY YOURSELF

My final suggestion is less of a technique and more of a way of life.

We *have to take responsibility for ourselves.*

This is a theme that has been running throughout my book, from my own childhood, through my ideas about your Whispering Soul and without a doubt embedded in all of the tips and techniques I have shared in this section. Taking responsibility is an absolutely key principle on which we have to live our life.

If we don't take charge of ourselves, then we cannot move on and nobody can make these changes for us. We have to do it ourselves and this means we have to be able to forgive ourselves. Without forgiveness, there can be no healing. Forgiveness is the core to all our healing. Do not accept unacceptable behaviour. However, forgiveness is where we can all get our healing from. What do I mean by that? Let me rewind to when my father was dying. If you recall, after my father's last visit in Bray when I was just 12, I didn't see him again for a long time. We hadn't seen him for nearly eleven years when a nurse in an English hospital rang us to say my father was in a ward there and was dying. She had found his marriage certificate – he'd told her he wasn't married. I went over to visit because I wanted to give him a chance to acknowledge and apologise for what he put me through as a child.

On his deathbed he said he didn't know me and he didn't have children.

He had a partner there with him, who'd been with him for over twenty years.

A beautiful man.

Obviously my father was a different man away from us. I don't know if it was guilt he had, or whether he just did not want to acknowledge his past life with my mother and us. He was dangerously cruel, mentally and physically. So when he got away from a life he didn't want anyway, he obviously allowed himself to become himself.

When I saw him at the hospital, there was no closure – he was still the same, he wasn't going to take responsibility. It was clear that nothing had changed. I left.

Now having said that, in the years that followed, he came to me, his soul visited me. However, he was still the same man, he wanted forgiveness without taking responsibility for the damage he'd done and while I had already forgiven him, he hadn't learned his own lesson. What he had to do was forgive himself.

Taking responsibility is all about us making choices as adults and is also intertwined in the previous suggestion about breaking the circle. Take for example a parent who smacks their child because they were smacked as a child. Or a parent who drinks too much but says their parents did the same. That's all very well, but how will an attitude like that help you change the pattern?

I've just spoken about the benefits of changing this pattern and breaking the circle. In order to do that, we have to take responsibility for our own actions. My mother drank and, sure enough, so did I; now you have come this far along my journey with me, you know that there were times when I drank too much and this caused more problems. But you will also know that both Dermot and I had to eventually take responsibility for ourselves and choose to stop drinking. Remember when we lost the house, the lads had to move school and everything caved in around me? That was decision time. That was our choice, our decision, our responsibility. It was no one else's.

Of course, it's never that easy to simply stop drinking, or stop being angry, or stop over-eating and so on, if that is an established pattern of behaviour. Each individual problem might have different causes and different solutions, but the point is until we take responsibility, we will get nowhere. For sure we are all brought up in different homes and sometimes those homes are far from ideal and cause us problems as we grow up. But we do grow up. We become adults. And as adults we have a responsibility to stop inappropriate behaviour. As adults we have choices – children generally don't, but adults do. Use those choices wisely and take ownership of them.

I tell all of my clients that until they take ownership of their choices and actions, they will not progress. I treat any children I work with just the same. I had one lad who was being bullied and was really struggling at school with his confidence. I sat him down and told him that doing his homework was his responsibility, not his mum's, not his dad's, but his and his alone. If he read better at school, he'd gain more confidence and gradually he would come out of himself. Sure enough, he rose to the challenge and turned the corner.

Taking charge is one thing I'd love to get across to you – because it is so simple and so empowering. Sadly, a lot of people are actually terrified of taking responsibility for their own selves and their own actions. But it's so easy when we do! When we listen to our Whispering Soul and hear what it is saying, we will be able to take responsibility and we will have so much more balance.

You'll quickly realise that life is so much easier; it's so much less of a struggle.

Your life will change.

So go on, what are you waiting for ..?

PART IV

CASE
HISTORIES

I want to share with you now a few case histories, people who have come to me for help or who I wanted to help. Hopefully, reading their stories will reinforce some of the specific techniques we've discussed as well as hint at other skills I use in my sessions, but also validate the life-changing benefits of learning to manage your thoughts. Clearly, some of the more severe and chronic aspects of some of these cases will thankfully not apply to the majority of people reading this book, but even if their story bears no relation to your own reality, you will hopefully be able to draw some inspiration from their tales.

CHLOE

When Chloe first came to me, I was struck by her beauty. She was so beautiful, but she was carrying such sadness and was completely burdened by her problems. She was only sixteen years old but was a broken soul who had spent the best part of a year in two different mental hospitals, because of self-harm and several attempted suicides. I could see her soul had totally gone out of her body, she was walking round just like a ghost, a shell. There was nothing behind her eyes, they were dead. She was being medicated and was also trying to come to terms with serious sexual abuse by her grandfather on her mother's side. Her parents had gotten my name from one of her cousins and Chloe's dad rang me. I told him I had to see if Chloe and I would have rapport; I always need to know if the person can trust me. If it's apparent they can, then I know I'm the person to help, but if not then I have to have complete integrity and give them the name of other people to speak to.

During Chloe's first visit with me, I realised straight away that she had totally disconnected from her soul self. I could see that no matter what we might do, it wouldn't work until I could get her to reconnect with herself. I began by asking her questions about her feelings around everything that had happened. During that session, I asked her to describe to me the way that she saw herself right now. Did she see herself as a daughter, as a sister, or was it just as an abused person?

I wasn't surprised when she told me that she couldn't see herself at all.

When you asked her what her own name was, it was almost as if she might not be able to tell you.

However, from the very first minute, I knew if she spent time with me it would work out.

I also knew it was going to take months.

Right from that first moment, we had to dismantle everything that had happened to her in the mental institutions, before we started rebuilding, but most importantly of all, I needed to bring her soul back into her body. I suggested to Chloe that she begin to listen for the whispers of her soul within, as this was her authentic self and would not guide her the wrong way.

The problem was, at this point she had absolutely no idea who she was, or even what she was and she had totally disconnected from her family. There was just no connection with Mum and Dad, even though they were great with her, she'd just gone from them.

We talked for an hour and half on that first day. I did explain she'd have to do the work, it wasn't me doing the work and there would be parts when she'd be very uncomfortable and she'd be very angry. I could see Chloe's soul, just sitting behind her and you could see the vibrant kid that was going to come back with the right help. She was such a beautiful little soul, I knew we could make it work for her because despite everything, I could also sense that if there was one emotion left, one clear thought or feeling remaining in her, it was the wish to get well. She probably wouldn't even have said this out loud herself, she was in such a bad way, but I could sense that deep inside she wanted to get well again.

I started with her signing an agreement with me that she wouldn't self-harm. We spent about 40 minutes on that. I explained also that she had to work with me, there had to be the desire to get better and that I would always be on my mobile. During that time, I got a clear insight into who Chloe really was, the girl that had been lost.

I knew she would want to self-harm again, she wasn't going to just stop. In my opinion, people self-harm to relieve themselves from pain, it's a way of controlling something in their life, the way some might control it with food and anorexia. When they actually cut and they feel the blood coming out, it gives them some release instead of tension and fear. It actually makes them feel in control.

I explained that I was going to give her tools that would provide her with the same release as self-harming. The first tool was an affirmation which went something along the lines of 'I can hear myself without harming myself and I love myself enough to actually make the change.' Beforehand, the unconscious statement would have been 'I need to release some pain and be in control and so I want to self-harm.' What we did was turn the statement around and actually make it work for her, rather than against her. This was all about helping to manage her thoughts.

We used other tools including one I have talked to you about – Tapping. She was holding all her emotions in her stomach and this technique helped to dissipate all that tension and stress from inside her body. She began gaining control over her emotions, rather than the emotions controlling her.

After the second session, she didn't self-harm again.

In the beginning, I'd ring her in the morning and get her out of bed, down the phone. When a person is in such a state, even getting out of bed can be an obstacle and if the parents are forcing the issue at that early time every day, it can really get the new dawn off to a bad start. So I'd phone and do it for them. They'd hand Chloe the phone in her bedroom and often she'd be aggressive and angry with me, but I'd simply say, 'I'm not coming off the phone till you are up and dressed, so you can shout all you like, Chloe. Now put the phone down and come back on the line when you are dressed.'

By the second session when Chloe had stopped self-harming, she was using breathing techniques and visualisation to combat the urge to cut. Gradually she began to realise that she had a choice in how she dealt with her feelings – she was starting to take ownership for herself and her decisions.

She still wasn't sleeping very well but the sense of achievement she felt in regard to the cutting carried her through the lack of sleep.

I kept in contact with her parents all the time too, because they were going to be part of the process. They gave me permission that unless it was self-harm or suicide as an issue, then anything Chloe did with me would be confidential; if there was any danger of suicide or if I felt she wasn't being honest about the self-harm, I'd come back to them.

I explained that Chloe needed to be able to start bringing herself back into the family. She had been totally disconnected from them and wasn't able to integrate. I told them that I would walk alongside Chloe, because I didn't have an emotional attachment and this would allow them to rebuild their relationship with her. I suggested that they would allow her to cook a family meal. It didn't matter whether it was good, bad, or indifferent, the important thing was the act of taking part. I gave her a recipe for Shepherd's Pie and I literally walked her through how to make that dish. As it turned out, the meal introduced the first opportunity in a long, long time for normal family interaction.

She started making the family a meal once a week and her brothers joined in too. I also got her cleaning her room and doing the washing once or twice a week, as well as taking her own uniform and ironing it, making it clear she needed to be part of the day-to-day family structure. It was brilliant for them all; she started integrating back into family life.

I should also point out that Chloe discussed her medication directly with her doctor and only came off it when he agreed. My ideas are complementary. I work alongside orthodox medicine. I would absolutely not encourage a reader with depression to shun medication; that was my personal fear because of my mother's situation with valium. That was just mine. I want to make that very clear.

At this point, I have to give maximum credit to Chloe: despite all the terrible things that had gone on, she was very good, she really wanted to self-harm at first but she used the tools I'd given her and really applied herself. *She took responsibility herself*, she really did; I feel this is why she had success so fast. It took an awful lot of effort for Chloe, she was so brave. There was life in her eyes again, within a few weeks you could see the connection back with her soul.

If she was really teetering on the edge of self-harm, she'd ring me. If that happened, I'd get her to do practical things, such as putting a wash on. It sounds odd perhaps, but I'd ask her to put a wash on a one-hour cycle and say, 'I'm going to call you in one hour when the wash is finished and see how you are doing.' Other times I'd tell her she should go and tidy her room and I'd call her half an hour later to see if it was done.

Quite quickly Chloe began to come back into life.

Within two months, it was agreed she could go back to school.

At first, her dad took her there (he'd taken six weeks off work to help Chloe get better, her parents were amazing). For the first week, she simply went in to school, registered and then her dad took her home. That was a big enough step. Then for the second week she stayed for one class; then two classes; and before long, she was going to school on her own using the bus. Most of the time I'd be ringing her and her parents continued to be incredibly supportive and helpful. Within six weeks she was integrated back into school completely.

Alongside all of these ideas, we were also dismantling her belief systems, because the abuse had been suffered at a very young age, so we had to work on that which of course meant memories were being triggered. She even went through a stage – not uncommon – where she wondered if she was just making it all up, because she'd been so young when it happened:

Am I being awful to my family? Am I just mad? That was a bit of a brick wall for a while. Memories from her mother and brother helped confirm that, sadly, the abuse was no fiction. All the time Chloe stayed brave and got through it.

She started to socialise again without overdosing on alcohol, or without doing anything that was damaging for her. Slowly she was starting to integrate into social life. She was getting very good at listening to her soul now and so her healing began to advance rapidly. When we confronted all the actual abuse, she obviously still felt angry from time to time but I got her to write a letter to her abuser and then burn it.

After about six months, I suggested I start reducing the frequency of visits with me. At first, both Chloe and her parents were nervous about this, but gaining independence is a vital step to recovery. Gradually, the time between appointments increased, as Chloe learned how to run her own brain, be in control of her emotions and manage her own thoughts. You could see that she was no longer a victim and was becoming increasingly powerful. To help her on her way, I asked her to keep a Gratitude Journal because by now there were so many experiences she was having to make her feel grateful again (I was still on the phone and I would still intervene if there was a major problem).

But with Chloe, there was no major problem.

She passed her Leaving Cert with excellent grades.

She integrated back into family life.

She enrolled on a college course to become a water-sports trainer which entailed a bus and train journey every day, made some great new friends and loved every minute of it.

She hasn't self-harmed again. Not once.

She has done it.

I honestly feel blessed that people invite me into that part of their lives and that I'm able to walk alongside somebody and hold that space – be their Whispering Soul for them – until they can hear it themselves. Chloe has listened to her Whispering Soul and reconnected with her own authentic self. She is back.

CHLOE'S TESTIMONY, 20TH APRIL, 2009

I began to self-harm by cutting myself on my arms at first, but later I moved on to my legs. I felt a release when I did this but it was more so that I wanted to see how far I could go with damaging myself. I used to do this in my bedroom at my desk. Then one evening I went downstairs and told my parents what I was doing and they erupted with anger. I was about sixteen at the time. They took me to see several different counsellor-type people and then our family doctor, who prescribed anti-depressants. Shortly after that, I was on a school trip to Paris when everything became too much for me and so one night I decided to take every pill in a bottle of anti-depressants. Later, I told one of my friends who was sharing the room with me and she ran to call one of the teachers to help. A doctor was called and she telephoned my parents to tell them. The next day, my parents had to travel to Paris to take me home.

After that I was taken to see another counsellor, I can't remember who it was but it was a guy anyway and I felt that I made some progress with him in terms of the self-harm. At that stage though, I didn't have any conscious memories of my abuse. That didn't come until after our summer holidays that year.

When I came back I was all over the place and I was cutting myself quite a lot, I just couldn't cope and my head was all over the place. I was really out of control at that point, I was mixing with a lot of other negative people and I even cut all my hair off. Don't they say that 'misery loves company'? My parents were watching me the whole time, for fear of what I might do next.

I can remember sitting down at the local health centre, speaking with a consultant and all he had to offer me was a diagnosis of 'teen depression', which was probably the most accurate assessment that he could give, but to me it was just a dreadfully condescending thing to hear. I was so upset, because I was just desperate and I had all these suicidal feelings. Then one of my friends suggested that I think about hospital. I hadn't really thought about that up to then but I knew that I couldn't deal with it myself and couldn't bear the thought of all the pain and distress I was causing to my mum and dad, so I agreed to sign myself into a mental institution.

I can remember that it was a really horrible place. I was in a ward with two grown women, who were both drug addicts. The whole place was shocking to me. I was only there for two days and then my parents had me transferred to another hospital which was like a five-star hotel compared to the first one. Even so, I was put into a lock-up ward and I remember that people kept changing all the time.

The ward was a really destructive place. I remember one patient was constantly telling the rest of us how to self-harm when we were locked up and how not to get caught. It seemed like I jumped out of the frying pan and straight into the fire! I was sucked into the institutional atmosphere and I began to self-harm at a far greater rate. I think I was kept in there for around three or four months. I had three professionals working with me at that time. One would talk to me and then talk to my parents. Then talk to me again and report back to my parents. Also, I had a visit from a psychiatrist every second day, or so. He told me nothing but I'm sure he knew what he was doing (laughs). I wasn't sure what I was doing in hospital. I just didn't know what was wrong with me but then I began to remember things ... gradually the whole memory came back about the abuse, which had been subjected on myself and my brothers too over a period of years. It was very painful and difficult for me to come to terms with and when they let me out of the hospital at Christmas, I was very unsure of myself and frightened to be outside of the hospital.

It was around that time that my cousin, who had been having sessions with you, Betty, suggested that I should come and talk to you. I didn't want to talk to anyone else but my parents brought me along anyway. I know I was very angry and un-cooperative that first time but I did listen to what you explained about the way you worked.

The immediate problem for me now was to get myself back into a normal daily routine, after having been out of day-to-day life for such a long time. It was scary for me and I wasn't even sure that I could do it but you helped me set some goals to start off. It was harder than I expected though, as some days I couldn't even get myself out of bed. You agreed to talk to me on the phone each morning before school and · this was such a help and support to me.

I think that once I understood that you were totally there for me, this was where my healing began. You suggested that I speak to my doctor about coming off my medication, which I didn't want to become dependent on and once he agreed, you were available to support me the whole way through that.

You agreed to take a call from me at any time, if I felt that I was going to self-harm. I didn't know if I was ready to give it up but we agreed that before I would do it, I would call you and talk over why I felt the need to take that action. You had me keep a Journal and write in all the emotions that would come up for me. My dad had also taken leave from work, so he could be there for me if I needed him. If I called him, he would come to school and pick me up immediately.

I actually began to have periods where I felt happy and started to enjoy life. I was able to rebuild my relationship with my parents too but there were some friends with whom I shared the self-harming, that I had to part company with.

I've learned how to forgive and let go of the past. This doesn't mean that I condone my abuser's actions but I will never allow it to control me any longer. I've also found ways to use the tools you've taught me such as Tapping and my Journal, to deal with situations that arise in my daily life. I feel that I have a much greater awareness but also the ability to confront issues head on, before they cause me any difficulties.

I think the most important lesson that I learned from the experience was that life does not stop. The experience was a lonely one, but even at its loneliest I was never alone. The power to move on and make something of my life lay within me and through connecting with that power I discovered a strength in myself that I would otherwise not have known existed. I learnt who my friends were and made some wonderful new ones in the process!

It was an uphill climb but the view from the top was breath-taking. Everything I needed to reach the point I am at now came from inside myself and it was through Betty's support and the wonderful tools she gave me that I was able to tap into that.

Chloe

EOIN

When Eoin came to me for Reiki healing the first time, he had been recommended by a friend. As soon as he arrived, it was obvious to me that he was really uncomfortable and possibly didn't even want to be there. So, I sat him down and spoke to him for a while and he commented on how beautiful the room I worked in was. He was surprised by the lovely landscaped area outside the window and the big, old tree which stood there. He told me he was suffering from manic depression. When describing how the illness affected him, he revealed that he'd spent several months of almost every year as a resident in a mental hospital.

He told me that the real reason he had come was that he knew that his sister-in-law would have wanted him to. He showed me a picture of her and told me that she was one of his closest friends. I put him up on the couch and told him to relax. I said he could talk if he wanted to but that it might be better if he was just to relax. Once I began the treatment, he quickly told me that he was experiencing tingling in his body and felt as though the heat had been turned up. I explained that this was his body healing and he should continue to relax. After the treatment, he told me that he wasn't sure what had happened but that he did feel very relaxed and would like to make a second appointment.

When he came for his second treatment, he told me that he had experienced a bad episode but that he was able to cope with it, whereas before he knew that he wouldn't have. The session went very well and he had become quite interested in Reiki and asked if it would be possible for him to learn it for himself. I agreed to teach him and so he became part of the next group I was training. Once he had completed the first level, he was very excited because he could feel the energy flow through his hands and he really got into it after that.

Within a few months, the changes were so great that his wife and family were speaking about him as if he had returned from the dead. He still uses Reiki on himself every day and he's very happy with his life now.

That was almost ten years ago and Eoin hasn't been hospitalised since.

INTERVIEW WITH EOIN, APRIL 2009

The first thing it's important to say is that I never ever had a problem with my childhood. I had the happiest childhood that anyone could have and that's no lie. I had an even happier teenage period in my life, right up until my Leaving Cert and I made most of my friends around that time, many of whom I'm still friendly with even now. I had excellent parents – they weren't what I would call affectionate people but they were very caring. So there was nothing in my childhood, looking back on it, that I could say would have created my depression.

Things started to go wrong and pear-shaped for me when I made up my mind that I was going to pursue my friends into university. Not that I wanted to go there specifically, in my own right, but the fact that my friends were going meant I was going to go. So, when I got into university (civil engineering), I began to feel a bit of stress and strain as most students would. I didn't know it at the time fully but I knew it many, many years later that I was actually going into a situation that I should have never gone into. After the degree, I worked within the University for a year then I went straight off to work as a civil engineer. I was totally out of sync and immersed in totally negative energy, things weren't working for me and it was playing on my mind. I guess at that time the first traces of depression were just starting, they didn't come out but they were there.

During the years from when I was 25 until I was 31, things were a little better. I met Breege and we fell in love and my whole being was focused on her and on the business of getting married and it eased the stresses of the job a little. It was alright then and so it went on until I was over 30 – the marriage was fine, everything was fine.

We lived in a small cottage in the county of Hertfordshire, very much like where I now live; in fact one of my daughters was struck by the similarity when she saw it first. I began to be very unhappy though. After a new business didn't work out, we decided to come back to Ireland when I was 30. That was the first time that I got so bad that I wasn't able to leave the house. I couldn't even go to the shops. Eventually Breege brought me to a doctor and she gave me valium and I slept for two days. I'd no job, there was no money coming in and we had to sell the car to pay debts. I was really worried because I didn't think I'd be able to keep going. The doctors didn't think there was anything wrong with me, so I wasn't sent forward for further investigation.

Eventually, I got a job working in local government. Surprisingly, it reached the period when I was 38 when people started to tell me how wonderful I was at work. I think it was more personality than engineering brains but they seemed to think I was able to do most anything that was related to government work. I was sent out to Iceland on a project and I delivered a fantastic job, but a guy there would only pay half of what he promised. That drove me over the edge and I completely broke down. I got in my car and drove down the country to the place where my mother came from. I was calling into places asking if anyone knew where her home was but it had been knocked down years ago. I felt totally lost. I must have called Breege, for when I arrived home, there were two doctors and two policemen waiting for me.

The doctors certified me as manic depressive (serious) and I was escorted to the mental hospital, where I was met at the door by staff and frog-marched to a lock-up ward. Then I was put face down in a bed and injected in my bum with some drug and didn't know anything more until two days later. When I awakened and saw the bars, I'll never forget the thoughts that went through my mind. I got really frightened as I thought that I would be left there for the rest of my life. I believed that I had reached the point in my life where I was finished. I was 41 at that time.

From then on for the next twenty years I was readmitted to the mental hospital eight times. The worst part of it was the depression, the elation was fine. I could deal with that because I felt okay. While I was depressed, I was smoking 120 fags a day and I worried all the time about Breege and the kids. They were so frightened and that caused me more worry.

On the second admission in 1985, I was allowed to go home for the weekends, if I was stable and not too depressed. The psychiatrist would know if I was okay. One particular weekend, while I was going back and waiting for a bus at the McBirneys store, I had my back to the Liffey wall and I was all prepared to throw myself in the river. I thought that I couldn't take anymore of my life, when suddenly the 78 bus came around the corner and right then I decided that I'd throw myself in next week. I contemplated suicide many times but because of Breege and the kids, I just couldn't do it. I've had friends that have done it but thankfully I never went that low.

Somehow, I managed to hold on to my job during this period, I suspect it was because of the fact that my bosses thought that I was suffering from alcoholism, due to my recurring bouts in the hospital. In fact, I was drinking very heavily but this was to subdue the [manic] elation. It got to the stage that I was still getting promoted and I was eventually promoted to a major infrastructure project, which I really was not capable of doing. Finally, I retired on the grounds of ill health and fell deeper into depression. I was back in the mental ward by the time I was 59 and the depression was as bad as ever. I remember being so desperate on my 60th birthday, that I wanted to smother myself.

Then my pal Jimmy suggested I go and see you, Betty. I said I wouldn't. He then said if you don't go for your own sake, then go for Judy's. That was Breege's sister. We had always been very close friends.

So, I relented and I went to see you in September of 2000 and brought along a picture of Judy with me. You just said, 'Come in' and told me to lie up on the bed and you did your Reiki. I thought it was lovely but something strange started to happen. While you were doing the Reiki on me, I felt a huge weight coming off my chest but it didn't really hit what had happened until I was driving home.

I then thought to myself, that during all the years back when I had depression, physically it was as if my chest would close up and I would have this terrible pain. Likewise, when I was elated, I would feel like my chest was being ripped apart. So I knew something really big had happened.

After that, myself and Breege went to America to visit Judy and while I was there I got a touch of elation but this time it was different because I took to my bed. Normally my eyes would be wide open and I'd hit the streets, going into any pub I could find and doing whatever I wanted. Breege couldn't understand it because the whole thing was different now. I was elated but I was lying down until it passed. It was a mini miracle!

That was 2000 and now, in 2009 I have never had another instance of depression, or elation. It's been put to me that it may be because I retired but I know that's not it because I retired at 57 and was still suffering up until I came to see you at 60. My psychiatrist feels it's because he changed the cocktail of drugs I was on but I don't think so. I've got friends who said that I was dead for twenty-odd years and pills don't fix that. Another friend said that he never really knew me until after I went to see you, Betty.

I've often thought about what happened to me. You're unable to generate any strength in the brain when you're ill and what you need is healing, like what you've done with me.

It's my belief that people who suffer from depression are people that are susceptible to influences. I've always admired people who are strong willed. They have the ability to make the right choice. Choices for depressed people though, are far more difficult. They are trapped in a hopeless mental situation.

Even though I had forty bad years when I had no peace or balance in my life, I was just so lucky in 2000 that everything turned around for me, when I began my healing. I've had a wonderful nine years. I've got my life back and have a wonderful relationship with my wife and children.

So I would say to anyone in the throes of depression that there is hope.

There's *always* a chance that things will change.

Eoin

NESSA

You've read about Chloe and Eoin, both in their own way suffering from severe mental challenges. Next I'd like to share with you a case history that was less extreme, less harrowing, but insightful and moving nonetheless. Partly this is to illustrate the benefits of using some of the tips and tools we have looked at, for many different lives and issues – it needn't be just for those in and out of mental institutions.

I'd now like to let you hear about a case history that is not strictly just personal. It is about a career and an ambitious young lady called Nessa (you've already met her briefly in my Gratitude Journal section!). She had taken voluntary redundancy nearly a year earlier but was struggling to get a new job because of negative thoughts creating a reality that threatened to push away her ideal next career move. My help here was far more practical as well as mental than other clients: we researched the companies she was being interviewed with, looked up the personnel who would be interviewing her, really got to grips with the practicalities of her interviews. But I also worked on her negative thoughts – as you now know, my own thoughts have been one of the hardest habits to break over the years, so I was well placed to speak with Nessa about controlling hers and replacing negatives with positives. Here's what happened.

NESSA'S RECOLLECTIONS

I set a vision of the type of company I wanted to work with. My vision was that I wanted to be working in the field of sustainability, advising and working with companies on sustainability issues, working as a consultant and that it would involve some travelling abroad. I did some interviews and one company were very interested, they were just waiting for outside contracts to be finalised and to secure additional funding before they could offer me a definite role.

I felt confident that a role would materialise. *However,* at one stage I began to slip back into the past and began to fantasise about a previous job that I had done a good interview for and which I had turned down. I slipped back into thinking that 'a bird in the hand would be better than two in the bush' and began to imagine what life would be like if I had taken this job. Sometimes I would also fantasise about the job I left on a voluntary redundancy basis some months earlier and allow myself to go into regret.

Betty, you taught me about the power of thoughts, both good and bad. Deep in my heart I knew that this type of thinking was not productive and could keep me in a place where I might not draw in the job I really wanted to create.

So I felt the need to say to myself that my thoughts are really, really powerful, why am I focusing on the past? How about focusing on the present and on attracting my new future. It really shook me up. I allowed myself to say goodbye to thoughts of my old job and the other job opportunity that I had turned down. I thanked those thoughts for the purpose they served for me, said I was ready to let go, that I forgave myself and told myself that all would be well. I then focused on the company that I recently interviewed with. I used visualisation, I looked at the company logo, imagined myself travelling into the office and really tapped into the excitement

I feel when a person or company talks about sustainability issues. If any of the old thoughts came up I just silently said 'Cancel and release' and moved on. I did some of these visualisations while I was doing the dishes and going about my daily jobs. Another powerful act that I took was opening my laptop and rearranging the folder where I kept my job applications. I put all of my past applications into one folder (which included the one I had turned down) and left all my current applications to the front − so that I would see the future possibilities.

About an hour or two after having completed this exercise, I got a phone call from the sustainability consultancy asking me if I would be interested in working with them on a project.

Changing our mindsets really does work and I am amazed how straightforward it was to do. I thought it would require lots of energy (it doesn't) and consume a good bit of time (again, it doesn't). A big help was repeating the exercise on a frequent basis, recognising when I was slipping.

Nessa

GERRY

My penultimate 'case history' is not actually a client at all.

It's my beautiful middle son, Gerry. I want to include his story here – which he has very bravely and very kindly said he is happy for me to tell – because it covers several of the techniques we have touched upon, but also because the extent to which he has taken responsibility for his own actions is a shining example of how to turn your life around. Am I biased because I'm his mum? Of course I am. Seriously though, Gerry has learned many hard lessons in the past eighteen months; listening to his story can hopefully teach many other people too.

We were aware that from the age of around 17 that Gerry was smoking marijuana. Dermot and I really did challenge him with his smoking although to be fair, in the first few years he did seem to have some degree of balance with it. As a parent, it is a very difficult phase when your children are grown up enough to make their own choices – many of which you may not agree with, but you have to let them find their own way. You simply have less control and less involvement in their lives.

Gerry left home around the age of 18 and after that he got more into the smoking. Over a short while, we did start to see him less frequently, until eventually we'd phone him up and say, 'You are coming out for lunch with us whether you like it or not! It's been a month since we last saw you, Gerry!'

I personally felt that Gerry's blueprint meant that he would stop smoking the drug at some point but I also knew that he would do it when he was ready, not when I told him. We just kept an eye on him and let him know that we were there for him if we were needed.

What we didn't know at the time and have only recently found out is that he had also gotten himself into daily cocaine use.

Then he got caught by the police.

He rang me himself to tell me what had happened.

I was gutted.

I'm a mother, I was devastated. This was Gerry, my floating spirit, I knew about his marijuana but I never thought he'd get in as deep as he did.

He came round the house and sat down to explain in more detail what had happened. He said that he'd only started taking cocaine socially at weekends at first, but that over time it became a habit and now he was unable to function without it. It had escalated and he ended up buying and selling it on because he had no money to feed his own habit ... and that's when he got caught by the police. This was obviously very hard for myself and Dermot to hear.

Gerry was extremely honest. He put up his hand and said that he made choices that he knew were wrong, that it was not our fault, that there was no blame to be handed out, it was his choice. We started to realise the various times when he'd obviously been using the drug. For example, on several occasions we would arrange to go round his house for lunch and maybe an hour before he'd ring and say he couldn't make it, something had come up. He apologised for this and said that if he had just taken cocaine, then he knew that we would probably pick up on that if we saw him face to face. He said that old friends had warned him he was getting in too deep and that they were concerned for him – Gerry is an amazing loveable young man, a gorgeous soul and people were concerned – but he had continued to make choices and those choices were wrong. He knew all of this, in a way there was nothing to tell him that he didn't already know. Gerry has told me he knew he was crossing the line but still did it, then he got to a stage where he didn't know how to stop. When we talked he said, 'I am actually relieved that I was caught.' He could have died in the drug system and there was for many months the possibility of a jail sentence hanging over his head, but he was adamant it was all for the best: 'I knew the way I was living was not the way you brought me up to live, Mum,' he said to me one day, 'and it's not the way I want to live in the future.'

To his great credit, he had also held his hands up to the detectives who had arrested him. He made no excuses and said it was his own choice. So already he was taking responsibility for himself instead of blaming others. We sat him down and got the other two lads around and explained what had gone on. I said that we had to come together as a family and support Gerry moving forward.

Gerry decided he was going to go cold turkey and we backed him 100%.

I asked that he move back home with us and that he do the cold turkey there. He agreed and I have to say I was delighted to have him home! I'm his mother! We hadn't seen his own place for a while but when we did it was dreadful, I said, 'Gerry, you can't live like this!' He protected us from that side of his life, he wouldn't let us in to his house so he'd come down the road and meet us.

I told him we were all behind him.

'There are a lot of changes you're going to have to make, Gerry,' I said. 'It's going to be the toughest thing you've ever done, it's going to be a *huge* challenge.'

And he just looked at me and said, 'Mum, I want this to stop. I have been asking whoever is up there to get me out of this but I didn't know how. Getting caught was the best thing that happened to me and there are consequences I've got to face. I've broken the law and I knew I was doing it and I'll take the consequences but I'm going to make this work for me. I want my life back, Mum.'

He came home and started the cold turkey straight away.

As a mother I took a couple of days and I fell apart. I decided I was going to give myself 48 hours, I knew I'd need at least that to deal with this before I could come back on board. I know I've said your Time Out might be fifteen minutes, maybe half an hour, but this was far more serious. I'll be honest, I felt sorry for myself, I questioned my own parenting, I cried for Gerry, for the boys and cried because I didn't know what his arrest was going to bring to us as a family.

When the 48 hours of my Time Out ended, to the minute, I came back on board. It was the only way to deal with it and avoid escalating into self-pity and that would have been no use to Gerry at all. So on the dot, I said to myself, *Right, Betty, you've done all your whinging and feeling sorry for yourself, how are you going to be here for Gerry as a parent? That's what your job is now, how can you do that?*

I am very proud of how we supported Gerry as a family. How we got through it was with communication. Fran came on board to support him, he started ringing him and came home as much as his work would allow. Adam's the same, he'd go for lunch with Gerry and pick him up from work. Dermot too, we all talked to him and asked him how he was feeling, what was happening in his body, we refused to get into blame and shame and just kept helping him focus on moving forward and getting better. We came closer together and the boys were a great support – they love him to bits and they love each other.

On a practical level during the cold turkey, we made him lots of hot soups and I made sure he was taking food in, made sure he was drinking plenty of water and encouraged him to get as much sleep as he could when it was possible. I got a music system and a television in his bedroom so there were plenty of distractions if he was having a difficult hour or day. The music was very helpful for getting him to sleep. At first, his brain wouldn't function, he literally couldn't think straight so we had to keep his mind occupied in ways he could manage.

The plan was to get him physically off the drugs and then to get him counselling away from me and the home. I felt it was important that he speak to someone other than his mother about his reality and what had happened. After just over three weeks he was off the drugs and then agreed to go to a counsellor. At first we found it very difficult to get a doctor to take him on and be supportive. Eventually we found a wonderful doctor who offered to help and this made a massive difference to Gerry's recovery. He agreed to weekly urine tests – I insisted on that – and he breezed through every one.

Of course, there were legal consequences for what he had done and during this time he was also in court on regular occasions heading towards a trial. The doctor was fabulous, her letters to the court were really supportive and the fact he freely submitted to urine tests helped too. Eventually, after eighteen months of uncertainty, he was handed a suspended sentence and community service. After the case, we spoke to one of the detectives who'd been on Gerry's particular case and we thanked him for the way they'd dealt with our son. He said, 'Do you know what? We like him, he's a likeable young man, he just needed a kick up the arse.'

He did go to the counselling and there were many parts of that he found useful. One afternoon though, he came back and told me that they had been talking in the session about childhoods and how so much of your childhood can affect your adulthood. Do you know what he said when they asked him about his childhood?

He said, 'I laughed and danced as a child.'

It's true. Gerry was the happiest child you'd ever see, always smiling. I used to say, 'I'll never have to worry about Gerry, he's so intelligent, so outgoing, I only ever see him smiling.' He loved learning and he needed very little as a kid.

When he was young and I'd be buying them toys, he'd say, 'I don't need that, Mum, I'm grand.'

He insisted that although we had moved house a lot and there had been money worries, he had still thoroughly enjoyed his childhood. 'Please don't think you ever let me down, Mum,' he'd said. 'I had the same upbringing as the lads, I have just made very bad choices. I made friends, I played football, you baked cakes and we all sat down to dinner and went to the park. This is not about my childhood, it is about my choices as an adult.'

Once we had got his head clear, he started reading again, which was something he hadn't done in years. This stimulated his mind again and he really started to recover. He started walking too, and to our delight he's totally back with his old friends who are not drug-related. Because Gerry's local community is very small, they all knew he'd been arrested and from day one rallied round him to help, every one of them has been amazing. Some have babies and are married with very busy lives but they still made the effort to rally round and help him.

Gerry stayed in his job the whole time – despite feeling physically awful no doubt – he never lost a day's work. Every morning at a quarter to six he dragged himself out of bed and went into work, fair play to him. Looking back, I'd say for the first three months his brain was gone, he couldn't function normally, but after that period, he really started to re-emerge. Gerry is beginning to see where he wants to be in life again. The marijuana had sedated his brain, numbed his drive and he had lost that eagerness to look forward, to aim for a great life. The life he is living now is great, he's out with the lads on Friday for a few pints and a meal, he'll go round to his mates' houses and play with the kids at barbecues ... simple, lovely things to do. Just recently, he turned to me and said, 'Mum, I am living again.'

As I write this book, Gerry has really blossomed and done so very well. He's back in life and he loves it and he's very proud of himself. I am too.

My little Gerry, my little floating soul, has come back to me.

THE GIRL FROM
THE HANDBAG FACTORY

You already know my final case history.

It's me, Betty Cosgrave.

During the writing of this book I suffered a very bad episode. Obviously the process of writing this and recalling events from my life – both good and bad – was very tiring, it was quite a shock how exhausted I was throughout the process. At first, I just slept heavily and assumed I was just tired, but it transpired that the book was actually taking more of a toll than I had at first realised. Coincidentally, the weather while I was writing was very sunny, it was brilliant sunshine for a period of about ten days before I started to feel something was wrong. For many people, the autumn can trigger depression as there is less sunlight and the poorer weather has a negative impact; for me, it's always been the opposite, because certain events in my life were during the bright summer months, so this good weather can trigger depression for me. As a child, the months from April till September were always very difficult because there were more hours in the day and quite often there may not have been adults around. I felt the longer days, there were more hours to fill, to take care of myself, to entertain myself, to cope. I found the hours between about 4pm and 8pm especially difficult, I'd want to close all the curtains at 4pm and just shut myself away.

The longer days and intense heat went on and it got hotter and hotter and I could really feel myself dipping. The combination of triggering my cellular memory for the book and the sunny weather eventually hit me hard. I sensed that the depression was creeping up on me – after all these years I am pretty sharp at reading the signs. So I'd already used a few tools, gratitude, eating well, breathing and so on, making sure I took time out of my day to listen to my soul even if I had to rearrange a few meetings, sleeping well, meditation, just using many of the ideas I've shared with you to keep myself in balance. I would also usually go to the sea. I'd drive out to Greystones, it's only about a 25-minute drive and I'd take a nice long walk by the sea and it all appeared to be balancing me out.

However, the actual episode itself almost came out of the blue.

I went to buy some flowers and it hit me like a juggernaut. Instantly.

I buy myself fresh flowers every week, it's a beautiful little habit to get into, they smell lovely and it's just a nice thing to see in your house. I have a huge beautiful room in the middle of the house and when you walk into it there's a square marble table in one corner and I have a very tall glass for flowers. I often put a Bird of Paradise or some grasses in it, I love having fresh flowers in my house. Not least because smells can be one of my triggers.

But on this particular day, before I could get to the flower shop, after about ten minutes of driving … BOOM!

I was gone.

It was almost like I was out of my body again, but I knew where I was and what was going on. As I began to come back, I was very panicky and started to shake, and a total panic overwhelmed me within seconds. There was a severe tension in my head. This all happened in a few seconds but I managed to pull the car over, fortunately there was a little industrial estate on my left so I was able to safely park up. Then all the smells came in and I couldn't breathe. I opened the windows of the car to get the smells out. There weren't literally any smells, of course, but as far as I was concerned there was and I felt sick because of them. I had a small bottle of water luckily, so I sipped from that too. The problem with the bad smells is you don't want to breathe them in, you want to hold your nose and keep the smell out – but of course that's the very last thing you should be doing, you should be breathing, controlling the oxygen in your blood, helping yourself with the simplest tool of all.

I could hear the voices in my head again too and they were babbling insanities at me, it was in my right brain, then my left, it was awful. I hadn't had that in many, many years so it was a real shock to hear again. Scary, in fact. It's actually my own voice talking about all the terrible things I am and can do, absolutely insane thoughts, horrible.

I sat in the car and immediately began deep breathing. I slowed my breathing down first, very deep breathing right into the pelvic floor. Then I used some Tapping and visualisation techniques to try to wrestle back some balance. I pictured myself breathing calmly and strolling along the beach, listening to the gentle waves falling on to the shore, the seagulls, the water, it's a picture I use often and can visualise instantly. As I have said before, it's not the tools themselves that are magic but the repetition of using them. To be able to manage something like this when a panic hits you that fast, you need to have been working the tools on a regular basis. You should look at the practice as a great way of preparing for future episodes. Hopefully there won't be any future episodes, but if there are, you will be very well equipped to deal with them.

I kept reminding myself that I was safe in the car, that I was off the road and that I could take all the time I needed to get back. I obviously know I manage depression but it had come as a big shock to suffer such a sudden and damaging episode. I repeated my techniques and sat there facing up to the feelings of panic and when I finally started to come back, to recover, I looked at the clock and it had been 45 minutes.

I rang Dermot.

'Dermot, I'm in a car park of an industrial estate and I've had an attack, you may need to come and get me. This is the worst attack I've had in years. Don't worry, I'm okay now but I'm not sure yet if I should be driving myself home. Can we just chat for a little while?' I just wanted to hear his voice and talk about anything, chat away to take the focus off the attack.

Besides, although I manage depression, I am blessed that I know what my issue is. It might not be a broken leg, but I know exactly what challenges my illness will present me with from time to time. A lot of people are afraid to admit they have depression, and that's very unfortunate. It is stigmatised as an illness. But I don't see it like that. Some people are out there and are very ill and perhaps don't even know that yet. If you don't know what it is or even that you have a problem at all, then how can you manage it? So I am blessed.

After coming off the phone with Dermot, I started the deep breathing again and after a few more minutes of seeing myself at the beach I really started to improve. I could feel every tendon and organ in my body starting to just relax, to unlock. *Breathe in for four seconds, breathe out for four, Betty.*

You know now what you should be looking at doing.

It works.

After about fifteen minutes, I no longer felt a danger to myself in the car and to other road users, so I pulled away slowly. I felt I should still go and buy the flowers because otherwise the episode would have impacted on my day more than I was prepared to let it. If I picked up the flowers, then all I had lost was about an hour and I'd had a shock of course, but I'd still got my jobs for the day done. I was not prepared to allow it to control my day. Not anymore. To have gone home and abandoned the day would have exaggerated the episode, it would have magnified the incident, it would have controlled me. But I was managing it, so I drove off to the flower shop.

They know me well at the florist because I buy the weekly

bunch from them. Even the act of picking the flowers, looking at the petals, smelling their beautiful scent, arranging the different colours, it was all very helpful and relaxed me hugely. The lady in there asked after me and we had a little chat which also helped. It would have been silly to have said, 'No, I am grand,' because I obviously wasn't, so I just said, 'I've had a bit of a shock but I'm okay, thanks Mary.' I didn't talk about the episode because if you do that it'll make it bigger and lead to more problems. Then I took the flowers, got back in the car, sipped some more water and drove home to Dermot.

After all that had happened, I decided to give myself a little 'me time', so I took a couple of days off, just really nurturing myself. I took some simple homeopathy which is another alternative tool, you can get excellent remedies for all sorts of situations personal to you. It's pure and natural and I only take it periodically when I feel the need for that boost.

I had one day when I didn't get out of my jammies, and this was really good. Even though I was a bit shaky, I did some lovely things: I read a book, it took me one day and I read the whole thing cover to cover; I sat down and watched some programmes I wouldn't normally have had time to see; and I had lovely baths with scented candles.

This might sound strange, especially to those readers with children, but as I suggested in the section on 'Finding Time For Yourself', if something like this happens, you need to be momentarily selfish. You need to think about yourself for a while. Just care for yourself. After all, if you are in such a state, you are no good to your kids anyway. Rushing about looking after everyone else isn't going to get you any better any time soon.

I made some nice hot soups and just rested for three days. All the time I was breathing well, you need to flood your brain with oxygen. It's such a simple but vital tool. The only change from my normal life that I made in the two weeks after the episode was to be extra-aware of any triggers. I paid a little more attention than usual to the aspects of my life that help and those that hinder. I kept managing myself.

I needed to be at home to get through those few days of recuperation and then I started coming back and returned to my day-to-day life, started seeing clients again, and within a few days it was all back to normal. That episode in the car park was the worst I have had for about twenty years and it was certainly the most fear I have felt for a very, very long time. But I knew what to do to deal with it and all the tips, techniques and ideas I had learned over the years had worked.

In the aftermath, I didn't reflect on it for ages, poring over and over with Dermot, analysing every small detail. That just lets it all back in again. I just said to myself, *Okay Betty, something has triggered this but it really doesn't matter what it was, the past is the past, 30 seconds ago is the past. That episode proves that you have learnt to deal with your depression … Betty, you can manage your thoughts!*

AFTERWORD

So there you have it. It's a long way from Ledwidge Crescent to *The Whispering Soul*, but I hope you've enjoyed the journey.

What I have tried to do with this book is help you listen to your Whispering Soul. You now know how important this is to your life and well-being. If you are not yet able to listen to your soul, then maybe for a while – through the pages of this book – I can be that nourishing word in the ear to encourage you, guide you and offer ideas. But you will learn that you can do that for yourself. Keep at it – practise, practise, practise – because your soul will eventually come through loud and clear and when it does, the results will be profound.

You will begin to take responsibility.

You will begin to make huge changes.

You will take small steps that have a big effect.

So take what is good for you and leave the rest.

It starts here.

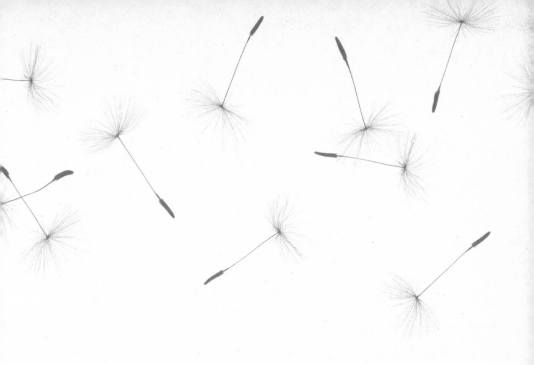

APPENDIX

Information about the tips, techniques and healing modalities referred to in this book, can be found at *www.bettycosgrave.com*

Further information can be found by consulting the websites outlined below.

KINESIOLOGY
www.wellneskinesiology.com
www.touch4health.com
www.braingym.org

NLP
www.richardbandler.com
www.purenlp.com
www.paulmckenna.com

COACHING
www.coachvillespain.com

REIKI
www.reikifederationireland.com
www.reiki.org

REFLEXOLOGY
www.reflexology-research.com
www.reflexology.ie

MY JOURNEY

As I developed my skills and knowledge over the years, I had many teachers. Men and women, who gave freely of their insight and wisdom and were extremely helpful to me. I have been inspired and hope in my turn to offer inspiration to others.

I would like to offer you all a very special thank you.

Olive Hayes *Reflexology*

Risteard De Barra *Kinesiology (Touch for Health)*

Wayne Topping *Emotional Stress Diffussion*

Angela Burr–Madison *Nutritional Kinesiology*

Pauline Geatons *Reiki*

Robert J Culpepper *Coaching*

Paul Mc Kenna *NLP*

Richard Bandler *NLP*

Michael Breen *NLP*

SYNERGY

'Synergy — the bonus that is achieved when things work together harmoniously.'
Mark Twain

Like any venture in life, the production of a literary work is a team effort and there are a number of people to whom I am very grateful for the support which they have given to me. Each and every one of them, simply by doing what they do best, made my life a whole lot easier. They are the sort of people who you would be more than happy to recommend to a friend.

Editor: Martin Roach *www.impbooks.com*

P.R.: Aine Carmody Smith *www.carmodysmithpr.com*

Website: Dave Henshaw *www.thisisace.com*

Design: Phil Gambrill at Fresh Lemon *www.freshlemon.co.uk*

Distribution and Sales: David O'Neill

Printing: *www.colourbooks.ie*

Photography: Stephanie Parisot *www.stephanieparisot.com*

Banking: Adele Delaney *www.bankofIreland.com*

Legal: Shelley Horan
www.barcouncil.ie/barristers/Ms_Shelley_Horan/3960/

Accounting: Andrew Noone / Anthony Casey
www.noonecasey.ie

IPPS LTD

A JOURNEY
WITH
BETTY COSGRAVE

Betty has created a series of motivational CDs aimed
at helping you reduce stress in your life.

For more information, visit her website at
www.bettycosgrave.com